NEW WAYS FOR INDIGENOUS
MANUFACTURING

NEW WAYS FOR INDIGENOUS MANUFACTURING

HOW RESEARCH REVELATIONS HAVE DEFINED A FUTURE PATH

JOHN FENTON

authorHOUSE®

AuthorHouse™
1663 Liberty Drive
Bloomington, IN 47403
www.authorhouse.com
Phone: 1-800-839-8640

Published by AuthorHouse   08/24/2012

ISBN: 978-1-4772-2320-8 (sc)
ISBN: 978-1-4772-2321-5 (e)

CONTENTS

INTRODUCTION

This book is especially topical in both the UK, and other mature economies, as wider public interest in manufacturing is clearly evident following disenchantment with financial sectors, and with rising youth unemployment. Rather than being an economics study the book's scope and content sets out to reveal the *discordant cultures* (identified by researchers) operating in industry and government, schools and universities, as well as the negative social and economic influences in UK and other national cultures that still inhibit manufacturing revival. The proposed readership will thus include opinion-leaders in all areas of public life concerned with influencing national culture in the direction of promoting indigenous manufacturing.

The book will have further appeal to social-science and engineering faculty libraries within higher education establishments, their academics teaching manufacturing management, and to post-graduate and undergraduate students undertaking related research projects in universities and business schools, interested in a *cultural critique*. The work's joint focus on national and industrial cultures, involving manufacturing-industry directors, senior engineers and managers within small - to medium-volume producers, will appeal to this further category of readers. Many potential readers are facing the prospect of changing the operation of their firms, not just to enhance growth, but to profit from new technologies.

New Ways for Indigenous Manufacturing

The book uses indigenous UK car-manufacturing as a case study, which also has a wide public interest, and is being subject to major change by its small to medium scale practitioners. This is in transferring from a conventional culture of vehicle manufacture, once crudely defined as a 'blacksmith industry', to one involving electric-vehicle design, development and construction, in the style of what was once termed a 'laboratory industry', being involved in both electric-propulsion and vehicle-control. A further objective is to widen the horizons of those medium sized companies in specialist-vehicle making, alongside principal companies in the supply-chain for motor manufacture together with larger scale after-sales service-engineering. Such companies might well take up of the challenge of electric-vehicle development and construction, by emulating the much praised culture of the German *Mittelstand* sector of her industry.

Previous publications about lessons to be learned from earlier national decline have principally embraced military, imperial and economic decline, the latter being divisible into its various sectors, including manufacturing, services and finance. Meanwhile most cultural studies of industrial decline have been, unlike this one, broadly focussed considering the whole economy, while some academics see the missing focus as being a study of an individual corporation at the micro level. This study incidentally focuses on one of the so-called 'new industries', which evolved during the slow run-down of the original 'staple industries' of the UK Industrial Revolution, and therefore has considerable historical interest. The study also uncovers the long-rooted bad practices that still corrode national and industrial cultures. It applies to a volume-industry sector dating from 1905 that became one organisation that was bankrupted and nationalised in 1975 before its final demise in 2005.

Cultural change for enhanced UK manufacturing

Solving the youth-unemployment situation in the UK requires expansion of those industrial sectors having relevantly high employment levels, alongside a growth in start-up companies that have arisen from recent technological innovation. While considerable progress at inspiring a new industrial culture has been made in research by UK management schools, many proffered solutions apparently fail to reach the board-room or shop-floor levels of medium sized British companies, which do not in general seem to match those of the successful German *mittellstand*.

During the Industrial Revolution many indigenous UK manufacturers were non-conformist (*dissenters from the state-established Anglican religion*) and were closer than their merchant counterparts to both the working-population and to the civic interests of their urban environment. A long-term mercantile culture had of course existed for centuries, alongside that of the UK's pioneering manufacturing economy, and had long been associated with international trade and imperial preference (*principally trading within empire markets*). At the same time the mercantile/aristocratic connection between them had been strengthened by the intermarriage of merchants and aristocrats (*exchanging pecuniary for social advantage; see below*).

Economic growth but not indigenous-manufacturing growth

However, an important proviso in the study of cultures related to so-called 'industrial decline' is that *economic* growth, albeit absolute and not relative, has in fact prevailed for the whole UK economy, since the start of the 20th century, despite the contraction of the indigenous manufacturing sector in recent decades. According to Collins &

Robbins[0.1] the 'long-boom', from the end of World-War 2 to the recession in 1974-6 (*when the UK indigenous volume motor industry leader became bankrupt*), involved UK industry, excluding foreign transplants, in relative rather than absolute economic decline for that period, which in political terms has been described as the 'social-democratic era'.

Despite the periodic decline in UK indigenous manufacturing the annual growth rate for the whole manufacturing economy throughout the entire period from 1880 to 1974, remained mostly positive: from 1% between 1900 and 1913, to 2.3% between 1922 and 1938, to 3.2% between 1957 and 1965. Annual productivity growth in these three periods was 0%, 1.1% and 2.4%. Comparative productivity growth for different nations is seen in *Table 1 of Appendix D*. However, the 'big-business' sector of UK manufacturing became unusually large, with the concentration ratio of the largest 100 firms increasing from 16% in 1909 to 32% in 1958 and 41% in 1970. For the US, the equivalent concentration over the 1960s period was just 30%.

Decline must therefore be assessed with care, in that an economy is made up of a multitude of activities and relationships, many beyond the national territory. What is clear is the recent erosion of the UK share of world trade in manufactured goods, the share dropping from 9.6% in 1960 to 5.8% in 1975: *see Fig. 1 in Appendix C*. UK percentage share in world trade of manufactured goods dropped from 45 to 35 between 1880 and 1900. The fall in UK share is shown for 1883 to 1905 and then onward for most of the next century. A continuous fall is seen over the whole period apart from the single rise presumably corresponding to the intensive post-World-War II export drive.

The public perspective is that the motor industry in the second half of the 20th century epitomised UK manufacturing industry's 'decline' and thus makes it a useful case study for the wider industry. By clarifying the peculiarly British institutional factors, and accompanying cultures, affecting the premature relative decline of one prominent indigenous manufacturing industry, this book highlights those negative aspects which, if reversed, might help to sustain both new industrial entrepreneurship and the growth of existing indigenous manufacturing operations. Such a process might also stimulate government to curtail foreign take-overs of those nascent UK high-technology enterprises that hold valuable intellectual property rights that are important to the future national economy.

Value of the cultural critique

Older-generation 'management-studies' academics, with their desire to restrict themselves to a 'scientific' analysis of decline, have been sceptical about the cultural-studies approach which can involve a more imaginative style of analysis. Scientific analysis has already provided apparently satisfactory explanations for industrial decline but the solutions suggested have not always led to effective reforms. Younger generations of management academics now recognise the usefulness of multi-disciplined approaches to research and already the 'cultural critique', of the type used here, has been applied extensively to economic decline at the macro level. According to Andrew Gamble, reader in political theory and institutions at Sheffield University, a respected analyst of UK decline, a gap is now said to remain in the literature for considering at least a certain number of institutional factors affecting decline, *particularly at the micro-level of the firm*[0.2].

The objective here is thus to examine this single automotive sector as a case-study to throw light on the factors that threaten the retention of a critical mass of general indigenous manufacturing that is needed to foster the technological research and development, for nurturing both the knowledge economy and small-to-medium scale manufacturing. The relevance of this project is evident in Gamble's work that addresses problems inherited from the UK's external trading culture. He argues that an anti-industrial *political* culture had become based on the: '*complex of attitudes and values which have created a social climate in England that has acted as a constant brake to industrialism'. The early 'industrialists eventually accommodated themselves to the social and political order of the ruling landowners'.* However, such 'theories' have the problem of vagueness and '*what would be most valuable would be to have detailed business histories showing how cultural attitudes held back innovation and the adoption of best-practice business models and technical processes'*, he suggests.

Financial sector superiority: over-a-century-old US/ UK 'problem'

Achieving the gradual rebalance of the UK economy, to advance the resurgence of indigenous manufacturing, has to be seen in the light of the history of the financial sectors of both the UK and the US. Current discussions in the better informed element of UK media relate to the differences, between productive and financial capitalism, thought to have their origins in the concerns of researchers and commentators shortly after the Industrial Revolution. That period coincided with the increasing centralisation and concentration of capital in the large corporations that had come into being in the US, which witnessed the growth of the crucial role of banks and financiers. The more recent near collapse of the banking sector in the UK has to be seen in the light of the beginnings of US financial capitalism in the late 19th century, at a time when former industrial owners in the UK were joining the ranks of the aristocracy, and moving from productive activities to finance.

Thorstein Veblen, a pioneer US researcher in this field writing at the beginning of the 20th century, divided economic structure into two divergent purposes: one of acquisition and one of production, being respectively 'pecuniary' and 'industrial'[0.3], which seem to resemble the current divide between the financial and manufacturing interest in the UK. However, in the US the timing was several decades after the first of the vast American industrial corporations had emerged towards the end of the UK Industrial Revolution. This was when a new class of super-rich took on the title of 'leisured class', as their founders passed on the running of their organisations to general managers, which was to occur later in the UK. Because the demands for the necessities of life were less pressing, for the well endowed and socially exclusive leisured class, it was the least responsive to the need for change and thus became the conservative class, arguably 'conserving the obsolescent'.

Consequently, Veblen argued that innovation became a phenomenon of the 'vulgar lower classes', the leisured class shrinking from it in their perception of involvement in it being seen as 'bad form'. This passed on to the middle classes as it became 'incumbent upon all "reputable" people to follow their (the leisured classes) lead', by using their surplus energy to partake in conspicuous consumption, a situation recognisable in the new 'service class' in the UK. 'Thus all classes, including the labouring poor, who were too deprived to risk any innovatory choices, had 'become stiffened against (any form of) innovation'. Meanwhile, industrial efficiency is best served by 'individual honesty, diligence, peacefulness, good-will, absence of self-seeking, recognition of causal sequence'. The phrase 'pecuniary purpose' is defined as conserving the predatory temperament and being concerned with ownership, plus the functions of acquisition and accumulation typically seen in financing and mercantile activities. Occupations that involved the production of goods, by contrast, had little predatory tendency but did of course have a pecuniary component, and it is noted that the discipline of modern life neither eliminates the 'aristocratic virtues nor fosters all the bourgeois ones'.

Trading in 'fictitious capital'

Hilferding in 1910 believed that the most important consequence was the significant rift between the industrial capitalist and the industrial entrepreneur[0.4]. A further consequence was the introduction of a 'promoter's profit', which was the result of selling shares in a newly formed joint-stock company for considerably more than the capital originally invested in the enterprise. This occurred if the yield on that capital was higher than the current rate of interest on investments. The phenomenon is treated quite separately from dividends paid out as a yield to shareholders and throws further light on the difference between ownership and control of production.

According to Hilferding, as this separation of the roles of industrial capitalist and entrepreneur developed, the capital invested in a firm became pure money-capital, rather than physical capital goods; the creditor money-capitalist had little to do with the capital involved in production. The rate of interest on this money capital is not fixed in advance but is only a claim on the yield (profit) of the enterprise. But unlike the shareholder the industrial capitalist must, of course, command a capital large enough to function independently in a particular industrial sector. For the money-capitalist a separate market, the stock exchange, exists for him/her to realise money capital on the share capital. Thus money acquired from subsequent sale of shares is not the same money originally invested for production purposes; one commanding market interest rates, the other commanding a yield corresponding to a portion of company profit.

Since the investor's share is not a claim to a part of the capital in active use its price does not depend on the value (or price) of the capital industrially employed. Hilferding maintains that the share thus seems to be a claim on part of the profit, making it variable in value, plus the prevailing market rate of interest. Because it is only the industrial capital and its profit that really exists, the 'fictitious capital' only exists in an accounting sense, being treated as 'share capital'. It is not capital, only a price made possible by every sum of money being deemed in a capitalist society to yield an income.

So turnover of shares is not a turnover of capital but a sale of, and purchase of, titles to income. The total sum of share capital need therefore not coincide with the money capital originally converted into industrial capital. The difference that appears in the 'promoter's profit', is that between the 'capital earning the average rate of profit and capital earning the average rate of interest'. It is suggested that control of the enterprise as a whole is in the hands of those holding a majority of shares, so a corporation can be controlled by those owning only half the capital, at the same time doubling the power of the large capitalists.

Mercantile culture and corporate governance seventy years on

According to Margaret Blair, the American 'shareholder-supreme' attitude to corporate governance (*how a company is controlled and its management supervised*), later to be adopted by the UK, reflected an example of mercantile culture ousting industrial culture. This was particularly so where the mode of governance failed to provide the long-term stability required for the effective performance of a manufacturing organisation[0.5]. It is suggested that, with companies engaged in takeovers, boardroom battles for control, downsizing and restructuring in the 1980s/1990s, there was reason to ask whether existing forms of corporate governance of the Anglo-Saxon pattern were working as well as they should.

This was particularly the case with markets for financial capital becoming increasingly global and where specialised knowledge by company staff was of increasing importance. Exclusive emphasis on the powers and rights of shareholders led to underinvestment by other stakeholders in the companies, such as employees and customers, and this diminished corporate wealth creation. Blair suggested that loss of industrial competitiveness in the 1980s triggered the US re-focus on corporate governance, particularly since 1983-1993 when this was accompanied by a 70% increase in the earnings of CEOs at a time of reductions in employee numbers and of imperceptible rise in labour-wage rates.

Even executives who failed to institute job cuts were themselves at risk and there was widespread employment insecurity, Blair maintained. The UK shareholder issue dated from the post depression era of the 1930s, and the separation of owners and managers, at a time when shareholders came under scrutiny, but was followed by concerns about managers being too attentive to shareholder interests, the result of which had been companies rejecting long-term interests in favour of short-term gains.

Defining terms: culture, business and industry, mercantile

The dictionary meaning of culture is 'the result of cultivation' and the dictionary-legitimate use of the word is to imply 'attitudes and values which inform a society'. Such attitudes and values are not in-born in individuals, or groups of people, but are 'cultivated' by the environments in which they live, whether these are educational, literary, workplace, social, leisure, family or even aesthetic. A divergence of cultures in the UK between those of the manufacturing and mercantile entrepreneur has arisen partly from the different environments in which they operate. In general the word culture in this study has been used in its sense of 'way-of-life' but in specific cases use of the word is adjusted as appropriate to the context of, and according to the prefix used for, the word 'culture'.

The word 'mercantile' is used here as applying to purely financial and trading activities (*the 'pecuniary purpose' seen by Veblen, above*) rather than to enterprises involved in making physical goods, which are collectively seen as 'manufacturing' activities. '*Mercantile*' is seen as relating to merchants, having to do with trade (commercial, mercenary); meanwhile 'mercantilism' means business of merchants or advocacy of the 'mercantilist system'. The latter is an old economic strategy based on the theory that a nation's interests are best served by accumulating reserves of bullion, etc, through the development of overseas trade and the restricting of imports, the impetus of much 17th and 18th century colonization by European powers. However, while the word 'business' includes the meanings of both manufacturing and mercantile the word 'industry' implies diligent, assiduous, steady action (usually implying manufacturing but can include trade).

UK mercantile culture has been described in many works of social/economic history as having historically elided with the aristocratic culture of land-owners and latterly this culture even affected the attitudes of manufacturing entrepreneurs. Under the 'shareholder supreme' view, within corporate governance, managers, also, become affected and often prefer to trade their companies rather than expand them from within. Mercantilism is said to have encouraged European wars prior to 1860 and led to imperialist adventures. Interest in mercantilism began to fade after the publication of Adam Smith's *Wealth of Nations* and the moves towards free trade.

The philosopher Adam Smith saw mercantilism as a conspiracy by merchants against consumers, within a rent-seeking society, merchants failing to recognise the concepts of absolute and comparative advantage. However, Ekelund & Tollison argue that the system further declined when Parliament gained the monarch's power to grant monopolies[0.6]. Now mercantilism has become a pejorative term associated with tariff-protection; China is said to be showing certain tendencies towards it, but some believe it an important temporary element in protecting infant industries, the short-term damage being offset by the long-term benefits.

More fundamentally, culture is seen by Raymond Williams[0.7] as shared meanings, the product of a whole people who have offered individual meanings, each of which is the product of a man's whole committed personal and social experience. However, he dismisses any modern interpretation of UK culture, which explicitly or implicitly *denies* the value of an industrial society, as really irrelevant. He suggests that the word 'industry' in the mid-19th century was no longer just a particular attribute but became a collective word for the activities of productive institutions. At the same time culture changed from meaning the 'tending of natural growth' to become a 'general state or habit of the mind': first of an individual and then for society as a whole, and finally a 'whole way of life, material, intellectual and spiritual'.

The new culture was not just a response to the new methods of production but also to the new kinds of personal and social relationships. Then, following the 1870 Education Act, a new mass-public came into being, which was literate but untrained in reading and 'low in taste and habit', mass culture following as a matter of course. Mass media was produced for this new public, not by working people themselves but by those, like tabloid newspapers, wanting to take commercial advantage of them.

Williams suggests that businessmen were defined as those who lived on business profits, as opposed to wages, fees or rentier income, and involved themselves actively in the business. The increasingly loosely-used term 'merchant' is more precisely defined as applying to those whose businesses were conducted from 'offices', 'counting houses', and warehouses (excluding the small number of early 'merchant manufacturers').

Production model concepts: Fordism and Flexible Specialisation

The interpretation of culture and history in this study is set around the concept of examining secondary data from existing research, and other historical/cultural literature, to reveal the way of life of different groups in and around the industrial community. Their attitudes towards indigenous manufacturing are thus revealed by cultural studies that help to explain partially hidden factors affecting UK industrial decline. In the view of Chris Barker, an early exponent of cultural studies, enabled the theory of Fordism (*defined below*) to be seen in its much wider sense as a system that affects cultural relations within society, rather than merely as an economic strategy[0.8].

Fordism did not just mean large-scale production of manufactured goods in the context of mass consumption but also a culture of relatively high wages, at least of core workers, to sustain purchasing demand; this was however allied to a low-wage sector of those without appropriate skills. Alongside was a developing culture of promotion and advertising to support sales and a full employment strategy as a means of boosting spending power.

Within Fordist production organisations, scientific management encouraged a culture involving separation of tasks, work measurement and worker-motivation by financial incentive, Barker points out. To maintain the stability of Fordism an economic culture included the domination of world currencies by the USA, some degree of inter-state co-operation and the federal state itself acting as corporate policy maker and economic manager. In general, the state created social welfare provision to keep people in work and was a significant employer of those with talents inappropriate for volume production.

By definition, increasing investment in mass-production techniques is one of the driving forces behind Fordism, a labour process involving moving assembly-line production and semi-skilled labour. Jessop's[0.9] classic description of the model sees it as a stable mode of macro-economic growth involving a virtuous circle based on rising productivity, economics of scale, rising incomes, increased mass demand and good profits from increased use of capacity. But Fordism is also a mode of social and economic regulation involving dominance by big corporations and a preference for orderly markets. Order is supplied by recognition and collective bargaining, wages indexed to industrial growth and retail price inflation, with monetary and credit policies maintaining effective aggregate demand and pricing policies limiting the role of competition.

Key wage deals are struck in mass-production industries, the going rate then spread via comparability claims and via indexing of welfare benefits for the rest of the population. The model also involves a general pattern of social organisation involving the consumption of standardised mass commodities within nuclear families. There is at the same time the bureaucratic state providing standardised collective goods and services. The state also arbitrates over disputes between labour and capital over the individual and social wage and the model is linked to Keynesian demand management and a universal state.

A production model more suited to UK manufacturing was flexible specialisation, successfully exploited in Japan, a process based on flexible machines or systems and an appropriately flexible work-force, defined in another work by Jessop[0.10]. Capitalists thus hoped to overcome the alienation and resistance of the mass-production worker by greater involvement in the thought processes of efficient manufacture and so reduce competitive threats from low-cost exporters in the developing world. Its virtuous circle relied on 'flexible production, growing productivity based on economics of scope and/or process innovation', together with rising incomes, increased demand for differentiated goods/services favoured by discretionary elements in the higher income sector.

This was in addition to 'increased profits based on technological and other innovation rents and the full utilization of flexible capacity', also reinvestment in more flexible production, equipment, sets of products and new organizational forms. Constant innovation was the key to success. The Japanese evolved a further their version of flexible-specialisation, as an approach to producing product-model variants for national markets. Their production model involved continuous redesign of the manufacturing system and establishing new relationships between assemblers and suppliers, also between management and workers, allowing minimum efficient scales of operation to be lowered. A number of the attributes of the flexible specialisation production model can be found in personal skills and team behaviour that were forming in the 18th and 19th centuries.

The culture of traditional British manufacturing

According to Brown[0.11], writing in 1965, the UK merchant/ manufacturer relationship dates back almost to the dark ages of English history when the merchant extended the markets for artisans beyond their immediate locality and held the superior role of 'distributor'. Merchant-gilds protected the merchants by wresting liberties from the feudal nobles and later craft-gilds were formed to protect the interests of the 'producer' from the economic tyranny of the merchants. In the Middle Ages a capitalist class of the 'captains of industry' type was beginning to emerge; on the other hand conditions in the sphere of human relations were often more satisfying than has since been the case, with social intercourse between the classes being much freer than was known in the industrial society of the mid 20th century.

Work was thus torn out of its original social context and 'became a hateful activity to be evaded whenever possible'; the employer no longer bought the worker, but just his labour without consideration of his or her health, or living conditions. As factory sizes increased during the 19th century the employer could no longer gather sufficient finance for his business so joint stock companies were formed that brought in shareholders and managers, alongside workers banding together to form unions. The worker was then regarded by management as 'economic man' motivated solely through pleasure and pain, the employer thus able to morally justify decisions in his own self-interest, workers' job satisfaction largely being ignored. Physical needs were satisfied but psychological ones such as responsibility, pride of craft, self respect in status, and a sense of social usefulness were unsatisfied. Widespread belief in luck in UK society, and the accompanying growth in gambling, has been suggested as being due to a 'society in which the fortunes of men seem to bear practically no relation to (individuals') merits and efforts', accentuated in situations where mass unemployment causes skilled and experienced people to depend on 'luck'.

Economic and cultural changes since the 18th century

According to the prominent guru of economic and cultural history, Will Hutton[0.12], said countries on the Atlantic seaboard saw the capacity of the elites to obstruct economic change gradually being weakened; but when warring factions of the elite classes ceased hostilities a significant result was that the resulting 'peace' consigned industry and trade to second-order activities that conferred little social status. One important stimulus had been the constitutional settlement of the 1689 Bill of Rights that laid down the path for stable political governance with Parliament containing members from town and country, merchants, industry and land, to represent all the elites.

However, in the second half of the nineteenth century Britain had failed to sustain the 'open state', the circulation of industrial elites, the renewal of public institutions and, above all, to keep entrepreneurship devoted to general wealth creation rather than protecting economic rent. The political settlement in Britain between 1700 and 1850, which had privileged the landed aristocracy and the Church of England in the House of Lords, had become obsolete and unwilling to make the concessions necessary for more complex economic development, strongly resisting any increase in the franchise that had been permitted in mainland Europe and America. Hutton suggests that the House of Lords routinely resisted any taxes earmarked to pay for mass education.

The Bank of England, unlike Germany's Reichsbank, refused to buy loans advanced to businesses that supported industrial investment, and new industries suffered the lack of productive entrepreneurs, finance and appropriately-skilled workers. Vested economic interests in the traditional industries and the City were too deeply entrenched for an imperfectly democratic system to force any challenge. Subsequently Thatcher, Reagan and Bush assumed the mantle of 'ultra-capitalist' but failed to appreciate what underpins capitalism's dynamism. The West thus became colonised by a new wave of monopolists, rent seekers and financial oligarchs that led to the debacle of the world-wide credit crunch.

A possible contemporary threat to indigenous industrial growth

Prior to the 2008 credit-crunch the decline of UK manufacturing, as a whole, had 'self-evident' causes related to the diversion of capital, labour and other resources from the industrial sector to the service and financial sectors. The recent experience of manufacturing migrating to developing countries with lower labour costs of course accentuated this impression of decline. However, it has also been the case that the substantial growth in transplants due to foreign direct investment (FDI) into the UK further draws attention to the negative as well as positive influence on indigenous manufacturing generally.

Despite their obvious benefits to the UK economy, such transplant manufacturing has been revealed to have led to some instability in the UK economy, given, for example, withdrawal in recent decades of substantial transplant volume-car manufacturing from the UK by such multi-national enterprises (MNEs) as Ford, in Dagenham, and General Motors, in Luton. It should not be forgotten, however, that Japanese transplants from that country's three leading makers account for a very strong volume-car manufacturing presence in the UK, alongside successful 'transplants' from the US (including GM), India and Germany that grew from former indigenous enterprises.

The British tradition of being an 'open' economy provides further evidence of FDI growth; while UK-born multi-national enterprises (MNEs) have consistently operated abroad, overseas manufacturing has been attracted into the UK through inward investment in transplants initially from mainly US - and Japanese-MNEs. These have sought to gain entry, via the UK, into the mainland European markets, but have at the same time captured a substantial share of the UK home market from indigenous makers.

In Hutton's view, from another work[0.13], UK officials seeking solutions to FDI problems *'never ask why the term-structure of British lending is so short . . . compared with other countries; why loan margins are so high; and why the interaction of British bankruptcy law and ownership system brings . . . foreign ownership'.* Remaining *specialist* sectors of the UK indigenous motor industry, and particularly some of the high-technology industries in other sectors, are also vulnerable to takeover by foreign transplants, as are the surviving British manufacturers of other goods.

How small to medium scale manufacturing might re-grow

The recent credit crunch, and the associated near-collapse of the banking sector, has directed attention once more to the UK's 'real' economy. There is again talk of the value of the manufacturing sector to the economy, thought of in the 19th century as being the foundation upon which the financial sector was built. By the start of the present century the value of the pound had dropped in relation to the euro and the dollar, which of course made manufacturing exports much less expensive and allowed a brief recovery before financial supremacy choked this off. There are also many other longer-term actions that could be taken to nurture the manufacturing sector, which have been learned from the mistakes of the past.

After perhaps the most critical task, of rebalancing the economy to counter high unemployment, comes the need to face up to the highly competitive manufacturing industries around the world, by attracting the very best brains in the UK financial sector, and the top universities, into indigenous manufacturing, so as to achieve a step-change in the quality of marketing, sales and financial control.

Many of the new opportunities for an enhanced manufacturing sector arise for *medium*-sized firms as many earlier attempts to revive *large* corporations in this sector have proved unsuccessful. A single concentration of attention to small start-up high-technology companies is also unlikely to enable the substantial job creation necessary to achieve reduction in large-scale unemployment. However, medium sized specialist indigenous firms in the automotive sector would seem to be well placed to meet the growing needs of both electric-vehicle development and other areas of medium-scale production.

Paul Nieuwenhuis and Peter Wells have convincingly argued for an alternative to the somewhat complacent view of a future motor industry dominated by half a dozen global super-companies[0.14]. They suggest that even if the world population peaks at 10 billion, global resources will never permit most of the world to enjoy anything like the 0.75 cars-per-capita US level of car ownership. Future business models are forecast in which larger companies should capture more of the automotive value chain by integrating assembly, distribution and aftercare, while medium-sized companies should perhaps concentrate on product design and research, intensive development, specialist-vehicle and prototype build, as well as pilot production for volume producers.

The seven major US, Japanese, Indian and German corporations building cars in the UK are very substantial employers, and now all have production models close to flexible specialisation that seem to be particularly sympathetic to the UK workforce, as well as providing a major financial input to the UK economy. In the first ten months of 2011 these UK car builders generated £22.4

billion in export sales and formed Britain's largest export industry. These foreign 'transplant' builders in the UK, as well as some smaller indigenous makers, produced a total of 1.35 million cars in 2010 (over three quarters exported), a figure approaching the 1972 record of 1.9 million (one third exported) for the whole UK motor industry at that time. The flexible specialisation production model has also demonstrated the possibility for manufacturing products economically in medium volumes to meet the requirements of niche markets, by such methods that lead to different niche models being built together on a common production line.

Worldwide, the automotive sector of manufacturing has traditionally generated jobs on a substantial scale, despite the high degree of automation that has been applied to that industry in order to enhance productivity. Although the mass-production of standardised cars and commercial vehicles has possibly reached its zenith in traditional industrialised markets, the opportunities for specialist vehicle production are growing in these traditional markets, particularly with respect to the growing demand for sports cars, electric cars and commercial vehicles. While some large mass-producers have developed electric cars (*as opposed to hybrids*), thus far many potential customers have been disappointed with the mileage-range of such vehicles; with desirable ranges having generally been achieved by specialist builders (at premium prices) such as Tesla in the US.

Main objective for this study

The decline of earlier UK indigenous mass-producers of cars has been largely seen by politicians and economists as due to 'malicious trade-union organisers within the factories' and the failure of manufacturers fully to adopt the US Fordist production model. However a number of economic and industrial historians have gradually revealed the importance of UK national and industrial cultural factors, as affecting UK manufacturing decline, and it is the purpose of this book to examine the works of historians and other researchers since the first (factory-system) and second (mass-production) industrial revolutions.

Revised opinions on the history of indigenous manufacturing decline, to be revealed in Chapters 1-4, support the view that the UK's traditional mercantile culture undermined the indigenous volume car-manufacturing economy. These chapters seek to highlight damaging actions by owners, managers and workers, as well as governments, which have actually thwarted indigenous manufacturing enterprise. These actions point to the proposals for enhancing indigenous UK medium-scale manufacturing prospects in Chapter 5. The intention is to validate the opinion of 20th century Establishment politicians such as Churchill and Macmillan: that the UK mercantile/manufacturing divide has been unusually wide and damaging[0.15, 0.16]. APPENDIX A examines one possible manufacturing sector that could reasonably be expected to expand in the near future.

Acknowledgements

The author is grateful to Professor Klaus Nielsen of the Clore Business School, Birkbeck, University of London, for helping to set out a structure for this work, and to Margaret Guy for proof-reading and general advice.

Abbreviations

BAe	British Aerospace	ICT	Information and Communication Technology
BL	British Leyland		
BMC	British Motor Corporation		
BMH	British Motor Holdings	IJV	International Joint Venture
BLMC	British Leyland Motor Corporation		
		IR	Industrial revolution
B of P	Balance of Payments	IRC	Industrial Redevelopment Council
CBI	Confederation of British industry		
		LBO	Leveraged Buy Out
CEO	Chief Executive Officer	LEA	Local education Authority
CME	Coordinated Market Economy	LMC	Leyland Motor Corporation
CPRS	Central Policy Review Staff	LME	Liberal market Economy
		LMH	Leyland Motor Holdings
CV	Commercial Vehicle	MNC	Multinational corporation
DEA	Department of Economic Affairs	MNE	Multinational enterprise
		MITI	Japan's department of trade and industry
DES	Department of Education and Science		
		NEB	National Enterprise Board
DoT	Department of Transport	NEDC	National enterprise development council
DTI	Department of Trade and Industry		
		PC	Personal Computer
EMU	European Monetary Union	PM	Prime Minister
		R&D	Research and Development
ERM	Exchange Rate Mechanism		
EV	Electric Vehicle	SDP	Social Democratic Party
FBI	Federation of British Industries	SME	Small to Medium Enterprises
FDI	Foreign Direct Investment	SMMT	Society of Motor Manufacturers and Traders
GCSE	General Certificate of Secondary Education		
		STD	Sunbeam Talbot Darracq
GDP	Gross Domestic Product	TUC	Trade Union Congress
GM	General Motors	WW	World War

CHAPTER 1

Lead-up to manufacturing by the 'new industries'

In this cultural study focussing on the UK car industry as a case-study, many of the revelations across the breadth of manufacturing, and the national culture in which it has to perform, have clear lessons for future indigenous British manufacturing revival. Cultural critiques of performance are beginning to be more apparent for indigenous British volume-production industry at the macro level, and many even for a whole sector of that industry, but very rarely do such critiques focus on individual corporations at the micro level, and still less on one that happens to become a complete sector of that industry, as in this example.

The years of the Industrial Revolution in the UK, and the years since to the present day, are examined in this chapter while the following three chapters cover successive spans of the 1905 to 2005 main study period, from the birth to the death of indigenous UK volume car manufacturing. The final Chapter 5 shows how the above-mentioned lessons lead to positive recommendations for reform of both public-institutions and the way of life of directors, managers and workpeople within indigenous manufacturing. This is alongside Appendix A, which deals with a newly developing specialist electric-car manufacturing segment, with prospects for the expansion of medium sized firms.

Pre-Victorian cultural influences

Researchers have shown that the occurrence of current cultural events often have their initial causes in past centuries. For example, a strong mercantile tradition in the UK stretched back to the country's international trading during the middle ages, and by the 17th century Samuel Pepys' diaries showed the mercantile classes ingratiating themselves with the aristocracy through acquisition of landed estates and the nobility marrying into the richer-merchant families[1.1].

The age of the merchant-adventurers was by then underway, in the period of mercantilism when government officials, military men and merchants 'exchanged social favours for professional ones'. This was also a time when both the town and country mansions of prominent merchants were matching those of aristocrats. However, mercantile enterprises such as the East India Company[1.2] had expanded as a result of military opportunism, as much as by mercantile endeavour, in the whole period during which the British Empire expanded.

The predominance in Britain of so-called 'mercantilism' (*defined in the Introduction*) up to late 18th century had prompted the philosopher Adam Smith to say 'every man was a merchant and the UK had a notorious attachment to trade'[1.3]. There was also a clear indication[1.4] that, after the establishment of the Bank of England in 1694, a gulf had reportedly opened between the UK's financial and manufacturing interests. With the reluctance of the banking system to embrace industry, the alternative source of finance for industrialists was the stock-exchange founded in 1773 to replace the 'jobbing' in coffee houses[1.5].

The lack of UK nationalist drive, that was singularly apparent in Germany, prevented the British from forming the partnerships between government and business that enriched German industry. Expanding empire commitments in the UK also restricted industrial advance, by redirecting capital investment overseas[1.6]. However, a number of more enlightened UK industrial entrepreneurs had joined cross-cultural societies such as the renowned Lunar Society in Birmingham whose members came from a wide area of the Midlands, and beyond, and represented a broad range of professions[1.7]. This was a new breed of men 'that did not see the world as a dying classical tragedy'. Scientists among them were generally out of sympathy with Cambridge's greatest scientist of an earlier period, Sir Isaac Newton. It was argued that Newton's, and other Royal Society members', views had had a 'catastrophic' influence on contemporary scientists who were into experimentation and invention, with 'mathematics becoming the new model of the sciences'. The Royal Society, by contrast, had become effectively a club for professors 'hobnobbing with the amateurs of the nobility'.

Downside of early UK national culture: an emerging 'coolie' class

The effect of national culture on the performance of British manufacturing industry has been usefully examined in detail by Correlli Barnett[1.8], an important analyst of the cultural factors affecting UK decline, who suggests that in the 18th century the British ruling class, 'squirearchy, merchants and aristocracy . . . saw foreign policy in terms of concrete interests (such as) markets . . . profits'. The Georgians thus witnessed a 'strategic approach to international relations' which after Waterloo changed considerably to one of 'moral liberalism', as a manifestation of Victorian 'romanticism', in which principle took over from expediency. Paradoxically this was also happening during the next three decades of buoyant industrial expansion, and comparative peace, when 'practical men' of the Industrial Revolution temporarily wrested some power from the aristocrats and merchants, but were also to wreak their own damage to industrial society.

The appallingly low level of education of the 'working classes', entering the factories at the first part of the 19th century from agricultural clearances in the countryside, meant they were 'at the mercy of a "practical-man" master who believed that the profitability of his business depended (only) on low wages and long hours'. The state of the resulting industrial working class was likened to that of 'coolies' in the outposts of Empire and were seen as the group from which 'Marx and Engels principally derived their conception of the alienated proletariat'. The machine was regarded by them as an enemy and technical progress as the destroyer of status. Meanwhile *laissez-faire* economic doctrine repealed old paternalistic legislation that had protected craft, employment, status and wages. Up to 1944 UK industrial strategy had been 'rooted in a Victorian mercantile conception of a myriad of firms competing in a marketplace - industry was still often referred to as "trade"'. It all helped to explain 'the appalling record for low productivity, strikes and shoddy workmanship which, by the 1970s, helped to destroy the (indigenous) British motor vehicle industry', in Barnett's opinion.

Establishment opposition to Victorian manufacturing

By the mid 19th century the focus of the Industrial Revolution had shifted away from textiles to civil and mechanical engineering, in the expanding railway industry, and was the mainstream of manufacturing for the predominantly male workforce employed in the sector. But this was also the time of bitter opposition to industrial development by members of the land-owning aristocracy[1.9] who delayed railway-enabling Bills in Parliament and fiercely protected their fox coverts against advancing railways, despite the handsome compensation payments made to land-owners. Lord Derby had delayed the commercially valuable 1830s rail link between Liverpool and Manchester, where it crossed his land, and the Duke of Wellington, as Prime Minister, while officially opening that railway, privately dreaded giving extra mobility to what he thought were the rebellious working classes as well as being horrified at the thought of a perilous future for horse transport. Eton College had even stopped the Great Western Railway from building a railway station at Slough, over a mile from the school.

Aristocrats also fought a fierce battle against Prime Ministers Peel and Gladstone to protect their farm produce monopoly against the free trade movement that had initially benefitted industry by freeing up overseas markets[1.10]. One of the benefits was the Cobden Treaty with France, which made that country reduce its tariffs on imported British machinery. But UK exports were to rise by 34 percent between 1840 and 1847 while UK imports rose by 44 percent. However, a so-called 'golden age' for British industry lasted from the mid-1840s to 1870, with the Great Exhibition in 1851 heralding its heyday. The only problem was that a high proportion of exports were going to semi-captive empire markets, rather than to the more competitive foreign markets. By the mid-1870s imports outstripped exports by about £70 million per year, at a time when some one billion pounds of capital was invested overseas, to the detriment of the future for home industry. From 1875 British industry was severely challenged by that in Germany and the United States, which had benefitted from improved productive efficiency, high import tariffs and marked superiority in technological education for a further century.

The passing of the Limited Liability Act in 1851 had offered some protection to individual factory owners and their business partners during the 'golden age' of manufacturing, it is suggested. On the other hand its longer term effect was to direct policy 'in the interests of numerous shareholders who never saw the works or their workers', with management becoming 'more impersonal and harsher'. By the end of the 19th century indigenous manufacturers had a relatively slow start in the new volume-production industries of industrial chemistry, bicycle, motor vehicle and electrical goods production. This was even to the extent of loss of market also being experienced due to transplant factories in these sectors being established in Britain by overseas makers. This was aided, interestingly, by the building of the Manchester ship canal and reportedly the first industrial estate in the world at Trafford Park attracting US corporations Ford and Westinghouse, to an area now ironically given over to football, cricket and shopping.

Malign influence of certain cultural factors

Capital formation was less than 7% of national income[1.11] (against the approximately one third needed for modernising advanced economies) at a time when UK overseas investment boomed at £60 million per year. The growth of business and industry saw a burgeoning of middle class individuals who early in Victoria's reign defended their culture against that of the aristocrats, but by the end of her reign many of the more affluent members had been assimilated into the upper classes. Expansion of the former medieval grammar schools into public schools was one of the effects of the expanding middle classes but, ironically, the culture of the public schools had the effect of luring sons of the middle classes into the leisured lifestyle of the aristocracy. Furthermore, communication between classes was stilted by the unfortunate trend of distancing oneself from perceived social inferiors, a trend seen in the upwardly mobile layers of the middle classes. That situation was worsened by the poor communication skills of British working people: a result of the very late introduction of free education in comparison with that available in industrial competitor countries. The resulting inequality of opportunity led to a loss in talent to the manufacturing community that might have contributed to better structured business organisations and improved management techniques.

In terms of capital movement, aristocratic indebtedness was drawing resources away from industry, because land was seen as a secure investment and land-owners were regarded by bankers as more credit-worthy than industrialists. However, loans of one and a half million pounds made to landowners in the 1820s were still outstanding at the end of Victoria's reign. At a time when the rural poor were moving into towns successful businessmen were moving to the country: the industrial middle classes who had generally lived close to their factories began to migrate to the suburbs and nearby countryside, many commuting by rail.

The upper classes, being defined by ownership of land, influenced the middle-class seeking to achieve a country-lifestyle; this was detrimental to the development of any talent which could have contributed towards industrial capability[1.12]. Though titles were commonplace they were no longer a badge of office; but there were historical signs of wealth creation by titled individuals in the prosperous service industries such as brewing, distilling and gambling. British literature continued to display an anti-urban bias[1.13] with writers painting an idyllic picture of the countryside, without reference to the hardships endured by the rural poor in earlier times: of labourers wearing sacks instead of coats, their wives with blistered fingers from stone-picking on frosty mornings, in a period when farmers were 'as rapacious as any mill-owner'.

Contrasting cultures of merchants and manufacturers

One explanation[1.14] for economic distress and exploitation of workpeople was that an artificial monopoly of the political system continued to be held by aristocrats and leading capitalists after the mid 19th century. Towards the end of the century class antagonism was most rife between the working class and those capitalists who were fund-holders, merchants and factors (*mercantile go-betweens for manufacturers*); employers who had more contact with their labour force usually had a better working relationship. There was also ill-feeling among workers towards prosperous merchants in the financial sector as a result of their withholding capital from manufacturing.

Respect for manufacturers increased with these members of the urban/industrial middle class being particularly admired for their contribution to municipal provision in provincial cities, while merchants tended to go for short-term profits, both in the City of London and the provinces[1.15]. Those directors involved in UK manufacturing in the 19th century were seen as having considerable impact on social cohesiveness and wellbeing as well as by their role as substantial employers.

A study of Britain's then second city, Glasgow, had revealed that although numerically a small part of the urban middle class, and a much less wealthy one than their merchant compatriots, the manufacturing section was 'a force for democratization . . . in a city previously dominated by a small, rich, and relatively closed merchant elite'. They were also widely perceived as daring innovators and noted for their foresight and hard work. They were often regarded as 'moral pioneers, philanthropists, and factory paternalists', helping 'to ensure the stability of middle-class communities'. In general the *urban* middle classes consisted of 'businessmen, professionals, non-manual employees', with businessmen numerically predominant. Manufacturers were just a small group among the businessmen and the one normally associated with entrepreneurship.

It was maintained that the myth of the manufacturer as 'wealthy self-made man' - in Dickens's "Bounderby" mould' - had no general validity in Victorian Glasgow, with only one manufacturer being of exceptional wealth, in terms of the scale of his will, among six businessmen each leaving over £100,000 in the 1861-1865 period. Manufacturers were obliged to make great *displays* of wealth with their family homes, since many were being used in collateral for raising business capital in a restricted capital market, which favoured aristocrats and landed gentry. The impressive factory itself was a 'stage of display' for attracting investment and a display at the Great Exhibition of 1851 even more so.

A climate of 'gentlemen and players' existed in business management[1.16] and 'the prosperous merchants of eighteenth century Leeds (in a quoted example) who had already achieved gentlemanly status, were not lured by the promise of profits into new and socially dubious (nineteenth century) adventures in manufacturing'. The so-called 'practical man' of the Industrial Revolution (who reputedly distrusted all theoretical knowledge) is a category seen as coming from the middle order of 'players': yeoman, traders and skilled artisans. Yet to an extent the leadership role exercised by the employed *gentlemen* (such as farm bailiffs in the countryside) had been *assumed* in industry by the 'practical men'.

The latter became anything from factory managers down to senior foremen but in general only 'gentlemen' could become partners and directors. From the layers of practical men a *few* directors might also be drawn who would *become* 'gentlemen', so forming a partnership of 'educated amateur' and 'practical man' at board level. This was one of the reasons why the Industrial Revolution could be seen as a triumph of applied technology rather than of *technik (defined below)*, or scientific theory. The directors' cultural partnership had gentlemen and players each having a built-in distrust of not just science but any theoretically based knowledge, including the new disciplines of economics, management science and industrial psychology; a huge brake on management proficiency.

An industry-hostile elite and a disenchanted workforce

Britain had been industrialised with a technology heavily reliant on manual skills, both to establish factories, and to keep them running, so that from 1830 to 1880 skilled workers were entrenched in positions of strength from which it was very hard to dislodge them[1.17]. However, by the 1880s, machine tools for the production of interchangeable, standardised, parts were available typically at factories such as that of BSA (*Birmingham Small Arms*) where mass-produced small-arms manufacture followed the US pattern pioneered by Colt.

The 1880s decade also marked the beginnings of large-scale bicycle production, when skilled mechanics worked alongside large numbers of less skilled workers who rarely advanced into the ranks of the former. This was mainly because of the introduction of standardised machine parts, which marked the beginning of the end of an era of predominantly skilled factory workers in engineering; a trend that continued throughout the fordist era. The resultant deskilling of work caused major industrial disturbances, culminating in the Engineering Trades Lock-out of 1897-8, damaging both the pride of skilled engineering workers and the atmosphere of industrial relations generally.

Most categories of labour were unwilling to absorb the values of businessmen or to put individual social mobility above class solidarity. New trade unions for artisans might have expected their members to accommodate themselves to a competitive economic system rather than challenge it. That they did *not* explained the rise in the number of unskilled workers' unions twenty years later. Even businessmen themselves showed only limited interest in the values they had held when they first prospered, choosing in many cases to be deferential, snobbish and have a sneaking fondness for the aristocracy. The first to differentiate between the worlds of wealth, land and industry, seeing the first prophetically as the most destructive 'senseless speculation, dangerous bubbles and the infamous trade of stock jobbing' was Trollope in his book *The Way we Live Now*.

Martin Wiener, one of the foremost researchers of the cultural factors affecting UK industrial decline, suggested that intelligentsia were the main critics of Victorian industrialism[1,18]. Their cultural attitudes were gradually instilled in businessmen, the rapidly expanding professional/bureaucratic class and the older-generation gentry/aristocracy. It was suggested that Marx and Engels had been wrong in asserting in 1850 that 'the only remaining aristocracy is the bourgeoisie' since from that time many larger landlords were prospering as a consequence of receiving income from railways, canals, mines and urban property and the 'geographically and religiously isolated industrial wealth' (*of the non-conformists*) was beginning to decline. However, like the nobility, the larger capitalist landlords were also to acquire land not to develop but to enjoy. The countryside was 'empty' in economic terms and thus *open* to newcomers and a migration from the towns of the upper middle classes, a move which deeply affected their psyche.

It was the key divide between the new businessmen which was important: between commerce and finance based in London and manufacturing centred in the north and midlands. The first group was more readily accepted by the old elite, the City having its heart in London, which was also the centre of upper middle class England and home for the winter residences of the nobility. The true industrialist was left somewhat isolated in a society which was failing to attach sufficient importance to the processes of material production. This helped to explain the aloofness of the 20th century City from British industry. A watershed was the failure of the City of Glasgow Bank in 1878 when the banking system chose to 'withdraw from long-term industrial investment' rather than to 're-organise so as to withstand the greater risks of steadily enlarging industrial requirements': a sign of the vicious circle of declining relative profitability, which was to particularly hit the new electrical and automobile industries.

Industry suffering from a deeply flawed educational culture

Resistance to both mercantile and industrial power came firstly from the 'small gentry' (squires), who had little interest in wealth creation and had their sons exposed to traditional codes of behaviour in the public schools and ancient universities[1.19]. Character forming was a more important role than the intellectual one, since, in this period, character was seen as a more important attribute than ability. This belief was, however, challenged later in the century when decline in the staple industries was accelerating and new industries required more theoretical knowledge. Public-schools had the role of mixing representatives of old landed families with the sons of the middle classes, an integration which gave a powerful incentive for the sons of manufacturers to desert their factories in favour of the gentlemanly leisured lifestyle.

New Ways for Indigenous Manufacturing

The poor education provided for Britain's future industrial workers was in stark contrast to that of mainland Western Europe where Napoleon had remodelled European law and developed the education system with the opening of secondary schools (lycées) and polytechnics for science and technology, decades ahead of their UK government-inspired counterparts[1.20]. Britain did not have a state elementary system until 1870, or a secondary one until 1902, starving the emerging industries of potential technologists and scientific managers.

For British manufacturing the situation was worsened in that more talented school-leavers almost always went to the 'merchant's office rather than that of the industrialist'[1.21]. On top of that nearly all levels of participation in the industrial society, including education, were reportedly misrepresented by the new style populist press that appeared towards the end of Victoria's reign[1.22]. It was argued that even social cohesion itself was thought to have been threatened by the outspokenness of new popular newspapers, such as Harmsworth's (later Lord Northcliffe) *Daily Mail*.

Meanwhile opportunism among the elite classes turned many old grammar schools into 'public' schools, by extending their geographical intake and providing boarding accommodation, excluding many bright students from poorer backgrounds who could have gone on to contribute to the management of manufacturing industry[1.23]. Any public school student considering an industrial career was usually steered towards the land, military, the professions or government service. The absence of free elementary education, before 1870, for those unable to afford school fees also meant that up to that time the labouring classes were virtually illiterate. There was a combination of lack of technical training, together with the continual influx of workers into industry from a failing agriculture. Such workers, moreover, who were ill-equipped to carry out industrial work and diluted the skill-base, contributed to the decline of late 19th century industry.

Unfortunately, in the opinion of British industrialists, education had not played a significant part in industrialism in the past. This was at a time when US factories were mechanising their production and thus moving industry into a more technological age. The UK skilled workers who had acquired useful tacit knowledge of their trades, as opposed to technological knowledge, were by the end of the century no longer the asset they had once been because industry was dominated by mechanics rather than the engineers needed to plan volume production.

In 1902 the rising Liberal politician Lloyd-George had turned toward education policy and declared that 'better education policy was necessary for the industrial and agricultural efficiency of Britain', observing that the country was engaged in 'an industrial war, a war of commercial supremacy' . . . 'we ought to train every man in the use of his industrial arms', the alternative being defeat under better trained countries[1.24]. To him education was also a means for reducing the class war, resulting in a better return on capital without reducing wages: such sentiments coming from politicians being rare almost until the present day.

In previously pressing the case for improved elementary education, Lloyd-George pointed out in 1891 that one person in nineteen of the population was in receipt of parish relief as a result of the lack of the basic skills. A further boost was given to his zeal for education reform by the 1906 Liberal election landslide, with 'corrective' education legislation given the first priority to provide equal opportunities of children from differing religious faiths.

The public school exception that proved the rule

It was claimed that the German concept of *Technik*, the process of designing and making things for the market, was almost unknown in UK manufacturing, particularly so in the Advisory Council on Scientific policy which later relegated the role of *Technik* to a second-class category of 'applied science' and the 'exploitation' of scientific discovery. Only the single public school, Oundle had adopted *Technik* as one of the foundations for its teaching. It had been said[1.25] that it took three-quarters of a century for the inspiration of Sanderson of Oundle, 'the last great reforming headmaster', to be accepted by the other public schools.

A housemaster at the school recorded the career of FW Sanderson, who like Thring at nearby Uppingham and Arnold at Rugby, was a major reformer of the public schools in the nineteenth century[1.26]. It was the governing body of the school at Oundle which had the far-sightedness in the last quarter of the nineteenth century to adopt a modern subject philosophy alongside the traditional teaching of classics. Sanderson had successfully installed one of the first science/engineering departments at another public-school when he was an assistant master at Dulwich College, prior to being appointed headmaster at Oundle in 1892. It was a dramatic precedent, for a mathematician rather than a classicist to be appointed and, what is more, a non-Oxbridge man and a radical Liberal by political persuasion. By 1911 the Oundle syllabus was sought after by County Council Directors of Education.

By scientific project work and experience in the school workshops 'the boy will learn his Mathematics by using them, in the same way that he learns to walk. Unconsciously he will begin to arrange his knowledge in some kind of logical framework, and at a later stage he will be taught formal Mathematics'. By the beginning of the 1920s

Sanderson was to restate the aims of engineering education: 'it is not intended to do away with the necessity for a subsequent professional pupilage, but rather to place boys in a position to make more intelligent progress during the pupilage'. Sanderson's idea was to raise the level of the average, or even sub-average, boy by demanding the fullest of his powers. He felt the same for the community at large and said 'there should be no soul-destroying repetitive work, dulling the mind and breeding unrest' but remembering that in a factory no one man makes the whole product, which meant that team-spirit was vital in factory and in school.

Nowadays at Oundle, under pressure of examinations, the compulsory week in workshops per term has been supplanted by a substantially new science and technology centre, SciTec, which helps to prepare pupils for the knowledge economy, while allowing voluntary attendance in the workshops.

Industry disapproval by the literati

According to a Cambridge University historian, one of the cultural factors affecting British industry was the 'Luddite interpretation of history', giving an important insight into the social and cultural forces which had constrained UK industrial growth[1.27] by appealing to 'deeply ingrained prejudices' in their readers. These attitudes could help to explain the career choices made by British graduates who favoured law, politics and the higher echelons of the civil services, with the 'consequential failure of business to recruit the ablest products of our society'.

While a disdainful attitude towards businessmen could be explained in terms of social snobbery, political hostility, religious prejudice, xenophobia, humanitarian revulsion and moral superiority, all these were dwarfed by the instinctive dislike arising from demonic accounts of industry given in literature. Dickens' industrialist Bounderby in *Hard Times* is portrayed as a vulgar, ignorant, self-interested liar. Even the utilitarian MP Gradgrind in the book was associated with the behaviour of industrialists in the readers' minds, rather than with the then contemporary educationalist, Joseph Lancaster (of 'mechanical education' and 'facts' infamy) whom Dickens was really attacking.

> *The contrast with treatment of businessmen in American literature (was) striking, where they (were) recognized as important figures in national life and (were) examined as such. In the UK (as in the USA) it was also realized that money was the passport to fashionable society but 'entry was easier if the commercial and industrial origins of the wealth could be disguised'. This is the (reason) for there being a paucity of autobiographical work on British businessmen and industrialists, together with their failure to attract the (positive) attention of novelists and historians. The position of UK businessmen has thus 'remained morally and socially ambiguous'.* (McKendrick)

Advancing towards the 'New Industries'

Developments of the early Industrial Revolution were technically quite primitive, simple ideas based on long-known technologies were often applied by essentially practical, but resourceful, men and produced impressive results[1.28]. However, by the 1880s when the 'new industries' were in prospect, those such as 'the manufacture of bicycles and motor vehicles (were) of a size and complexity (that) put them beyond the experience of most of the small class of local businessmen'.

New Ways for Indigenous Manufacturing

'It is strange to contemplate the situation of a country officially committed to a free-enterprise system, and its appropriate economic and political attitudes, with its economy becoming more and more dependent upon its business efficiency in a competitive world, yet with the educational system of the upper and middle classes possessing a value system that elevated service to the state and the liberal professions in status and depressed the status of becoming involved in trade or more particularly manufacturing industry. But the financial sector escaped this prejudice to a large degree' (Hobsbawm).

While US workers had clear incentives to earn money to improve the prospects of their families, UK workers were still haunted by the traditions of feudalism[1.29]. Attempts to achieve co-operation between workers and managers often failed because of the divisive social stratification which prevailed. This was at a time when aristocrats were enriching themselves by selling land for urban development and the sons of industrialists were becoming absorbed into the less production-oriented elites. Industrial towns were consequently gradually denuded of their opinion-leaders[1.30].

However, while the middle classes had nowhere near the wealth of the landed classes, experience showed that they had the skill and nerve to put their money into productive use[1.31]. But employment for the sons of successful middle class business people was not easy to come by, as most firms were not big enough to employ professional salaried staff. Poorly paid clerical jobs seemed to be the usual outcome, perhaps spawning the original lower middle class. Late-Victorian middle classes were less puritanical than their fathers and grandfathers; they tended to move from religious non-conformity to the Anglican Church. Non-conformity itself became less rigorous and a generally more relaxed atmosphere inevitably affected the workplace. While in the 1860s a 12 hour day was commonplace for all employees including office workers, by the early 20th century the forerunners of ICI (Nobel Dynamite) opened their London office from 9.30 a.m. to 5 p.m., with a generous lunch interval.

After 1870 enthusiasm for free-trade gradually began to decline and a return to protection and state regulation started to grow but this was different from the old mercantilism[1.32]. In the financial sector Britain's main joint-stock banks had been first formed in the 1860s and by the 1880s the number of private (country) banks had fallen to 172, with joint-stock banks taking over half the country's deposits. By 1900 country banks were insignificant but the consolidation of joint-stock banks had led to conservative lending policies, branch-managers' freedom of action being restricted by London head offices. The system became devoted to short-term lending 'without being an important instrument for financial investment', unlike the German system. As profits were squeezed by declining prices in the Great Depression, from 1873-1886, so investment funds in the export industries under pressure became restricted.

A high proportion of investment in traditional UK manufacturing industry derived directly from profits of individual companies[1.33] It was also advantageous that almost 60% of capital for 'new' companies between 1885 and 1914 had gone direct from private investors to the entrepreneurs setting up the companies rather than being by public contribution, with the intention that no outsider could control the company, only preference shares or debentures being sold to the public.

Export of capital from the UK was responding to rates of return possible to overseas investors which were higher than those available in UK government stock[1.34]. About a third of total UK savings flowed abroad between 1870 and 1914. It is argued that a greater export trade in chemicals, electrical products and motor vehicles would have helped the economy more than dividends from investment abroad. The 1890s was also to see a new era of constructive imperialism as overseas protectionism was beginning to freeze the UK out of former foreign markets. Thus *laissez-faire* in colonial matters had been abandoned in favour of imperial preference at the Ottawa conference of 1894, when the birth of self-governing dominions was taking place. Since companies were being traded in a market of their own, eventually a renewed 'service-class' of managers was emerging to resemble, in culture, that of the government's civil service[1.35]

Pre-World-War I UK motor industry pioneers

The appearance of motor vehicles in the UK in 1893 was very much a mercantile affair with merchants trading in cars made in Germany and France (and later the USA). No major UK engineering company had set out to produce cars in the manner of the French and Germans. A German-speaking UK trader, FR Simms, was first to introduce licensed manufacture of Daimler cars into the UK for the luxury market. Even at the end of the 19th century motor manufacture was a relatively small-scale enterprise, with cars built mainly for the upper classes. Another trader, Percival Perry, of Central Motors in London, was later to import Ford cars from the US for the middle class market and he was eventually involved, with Ford US in 1911, in setting up the transplant for the assembly of the model-T in Manchester. Major systems for the car came into the Trafford Park plant from the US, via Liverpool, along the newly opened Manchester Ship Canal.

This date was only a few decades after the gentry and aristocracy, with incomers from the top end of the mercantile class, were formerly ruling the country, while manual workers in the old staple industries were increasing in number and still having no say in their working lives or the layout of their workplace. Displacement of the rural poor by land enclosures was exacerbated by a series of bad harvests and large-scale food importation: so that men who were at most a generation or two from agricultural serfdom drifted into towns in search of work. Skilled workers from the old staple industries resented this intake of people unskilled in manufacturing, who did not even adapt well to the job requirements of the new industries of the 1890s. Both groups had been deeply embittered by the long depression of 1877 to 1886 which had hit both UK manufacturing and agriculture.

UK motor industry entrepreneurs mostly set up in the West Midlands region around Birmingham[1.36], where sub-contracting the manufacture of motor parts was possible and machine-tool manufacturing was flourishing; this was a city historically free of a controlling corporation and therefore attractive to dissenting entrepreneurs such as Joseph Lucas, a key supplier of components for bicycles and later motor vehicles. One third of motor cars existing in the UK by 1914 were imports and while indigenous car firms were run by reasonably competent practical engineers this had the downside of having marketing decisions being subordinate to technical ones.

However, 'technical' did not imply technological, and practical engineers were not technologists, science being recognisably missing from this early concept of 'engineering'. Proper production planning was hardly in evidence initially and mostly one car was built completely before the next one was produced; the adventurous non-conformist entrepreneur was largely absent from the ranks of luxury car builders. While skilled workers were available from traditional industries they were often less suited for future volume-production roles. By the 1880s, when the 'new industries' were in prospect, those such as bicycle and motor vehicle making being more complex than what was experienced by managers in the existing staple industries.

New Ways for Indigenous Manufacturing

Although, historical research has shown that there was some logic in pioneer UK car-makers adjusting to a particular labour situation that applied at the end of the 19th century. Then the staple industries of the Industrial Revolution era, and after, had been used to a highly skilled workforce largely controlled by master-craftsmen, particularly in the mechanical engineering industries, some of which later came to embrace motor manufacture. The opposite situation was said to have existed in the US, which experienced a shortage of skilled craftsmen, making the prospect of mechanized production with a semi-skilled workforce much more attractive.

The start of the UK indigenous motor industry in the 1890s had been largely in the hands of promoters and financiers seeking to capitalise on US, French and German progress by means of licensed manufacture and inward-investment deals[1.37]. At that stage only one large UK engineering company, Vickers, had become involved in car-making, through its purchase of luxury car maker Wolseley, with its chief designer Herbert Austin. Even that venture eventually faltered, though Austin was to set up on his own in 1905 to found a car-manufacture business that was in due course to flourish in the inter-war volume market. The new investing public in the early 20th century had often been misled by unscrupulous promoters, and sounder concerns suffered with capital becoming scarce as a consequence[1.38]. Many car makers had the disadvantage of being dominated by 'mechanics' and motor-sportsmen[1.39] rather than technologists and professional managers: 'the industry was quite unable to release itself from the traditional ways of engineering'.

Former agricultural workers from the land clearances were unfitted both for the expanding urban communities and the semi-skilled jobs arising in the new industries, while management's 'practical men', who had led the established staple industries, were ill-fitted for management in the forthcoming volume-production industries. Many

22

of the socially ambitious industrialists themselves joined the 'rural elite' of county families and moved away from industrial ownership. Upper-class involvement with the emerging motor industry was mostly restricted to motor sport, which attracted some to invest in sports car manufacture. Industry entrepreneurs among the specialist luxury car makers employed mechanics that could 'fit' one part to another, as standardised parts, and often blueprints, were absent alongside the culture of working to detail - and assembly-drawings.

Start-up firms had, moreover, become dependent on stock-market funding, which put makers at a disadvantage with their overseas motor manufacturers, in their susceptibility to take-over. Meanwhile semi-skilled labour, which was sufficiently literate and numerate for volume-production work requiring the reading of instructions, was scarce. Volume motor manufacturing was in any case late to start in the UK, due to the impediments of poor industrial relations, restricted public purchasing power and lack of a long-term investment capital. The US, France and Germany did not, however, suffer from such constraints, the US particularly enjoying a large homogenous home market that was expanding rapidly. This was in addition to a keen migrant workforce which was adaptable to new manufacturing techniques. European and US markets, meanwhile, were protected by local tariffs, while Britain's commitment to free-trade made the home market vulnerable to imports.

UK industry as a whole was characterised by the 'country-house' style seen in its company headquarters in the capital[1.40], the British inheriting their own tradition of paternalism and company loyalty from landed estates, or chartered mercantile corporations such as the East India Company, with little representation of the lives of more benign owners of early industries such as the Wedgwoods, Cadburys and Rowntrees. (Anthony Sampson)

CHAPTER 2

'New industries' start slowly, and expand rapidly, 1905-1945

Growth of financial capitalism at the end of the 19th century, and the beginning of the 20th century, was gradually weakening the enterprise culture of industrial capitalism in the midland- and north-country, as potential entrepreneurs from the elite classes were drawn into financial trading after leaving school and became aloof from manufacturing. Even successful non-conformist manufacturers were eventually drawn into this milieu. Early motor industry entrepreneurs tended to be motor-sport enthusiasts from the aristocracy, former cycle makers and practical engineers. Management training was largely unknown among the entrepreneurs and the investors were mainly short-term speculators attracted into motor stock by unscrupulous promoters. Indigenous volume car production would have hardly got off the ground without the exceptional foresight of Herbert Austin and William Morris both of whom anticipated the widening market for their products with the gradual growth in prosperity. Figs. 2, 3 and 4, in Appendix C show the production and profit figures for the major manufacturers, also for the low/medium volume MG company associated with Morris Motors.

New Ways for Indigenous Manufacturing

By the 1930s Ford UK was in another sense using a flawed form of Fordism, in that the UK market was still too segmented for high volume production. The graphs show Ford's early supremacy of production from its original transplant. This was when indigenous makers were slow to break out of serving the luxury market before getting into significant production volumes. Ford and GM-Vauxhall both reached significant volumes in the second half of the 1930s, but did not quite surpass Austin and Morris prior to the general downturn in production of all four firms, during the armaments drive and falling car market before World-War II. In Fig. 3 Morris's profit and sales appear to return to zero in 1934 after becoming a public company but in fact they later became incorporated into Nuffield Group for which figures are not shown.

While Austin had a better start than Morris, its performance lagged in the 1920s, during a period of post-World-War 1 retrenchment following its near liquidation, and then caught up with, and overtook Morris in sales after 1934. Not until two years after production started at Dagenham in 1932, with the Y-model, did Ford sales really improve when it introduced the 'Popular' model at just £100 (a 25% drop in price of its derivative model), which was to lift Ford into third place in the UK market. Small specialist makers such as MG, an associated company of Morris, made considerable profits in the 1930s up until the approach of war and could operate successfully at volumes over just 2000/year, Fig. 4, pointing the way to potential UK success in small/medium volume car manufacture.

Not only was the financial sector aloof from manufacturing but very few of its members, or their clients, had invested either directly or via the banks in the motor industry. Such capital as was available for manufacture had either to be accumulated from within companies or obtained through stock-exchange issues that endangered the long-term ownership of these enterprises. Capital was not the only problem for motor manufacturers, who had largely inherited labour control practices from the old staple industries. At the beginning of the industry highly skilled men were needed for elaborate 'fitting' together of non-standardised parts in the up-market cars.

However, the need for such skills gradually reduced as volume manufacture using standardised parts progressed. When semi-skilled workers were employed later on this was greatly resisted by the large body of skilled men and demarcation disputes occurred which continued until quite late in the 20th century. Herbert Austin was to partially alleviate this problem as he enhanced production by developing a highly integrated manufacturing plant, where skilled men also took on the construction of machine tools and assembly fixtures as the company advanced into volume production.

A national culture unsympathetic to manufacturing

At the beginning of the 20th century many super-rich merchants of financial capitalism, and indeed aristocrats, were influenced by the extravagant life-style of the new King, Edward VIIth, as were some leaders of the larger manufacturing companies and of the burgeoning service industry. In the inter-war years the astute social commentator George Orwell was to say that class in the UK was defined by 'a state of two distinct nations, with inequality unmatched throughout Europe, and upper fringes of the upper classes being identical to what they were a century earlier', middle-class people being 'graded according to their degree of resemblance to the aristocracy'.

However, motor industry pioneers Herbert Austin and William Morris, whose companies had also become quite sizeable concerns by the start of World War 1, had remained fully committed to their companies. But later in life, William Morris was either conspicuous by his absence (at a time when he was still Chief Executive) or, when present, paid undue attention to detailed matters which were more appropriately the responsibility of his senior subordinates. Austin's massive involvement with World War I munitions production and the lack of government help in reconverting new factories that had been built during the war, back into automotive production, caused financial turmoil for the company. It was thus overtaken by Morris in production volumes for a period in the late 1920s as Austin had been driven into near bankruptcy during the 1921 recession.

Across manufacturing as a whole, however, the British business class was increasingly being acculturated into the social pattern of the gentry as the sons of the founders of the late 19th century new industries inherited the public school culture[2.1]. Inter-class conflict ensued following the wholesale slaughter of the 1914-18 war, which led to general disillusionment of the working classes with the upper classes. Aristocratic and family influences also played their part in the appointment of directors in other parts of the indigenous motor industry.

The influence of the aristocracy and other wealthy families on small to medium scale auto-makers was evident around this time, when the fourth largest indigenous volume car maker after Austin, Morris and Standard became the Rootes Group, which had grown by the amalgamation of several smaller companies. The Earl of Shrewsbury had financed one of these, and his family name, Talbot, was used to turn the importer of French Clements into Clement Talbot, a company which was in due course to assemble these cars in the UK. Another one of these companies, Sunbeam, was run by Charles Marston who hailed from a Tory land-owning family and was keenly interested in motor sport and land speed record breaking.

William Morris was more troubled by his executives than his involvement in family matters: one of his key appointees in the early 1930s was a talented production engineer, Leonard Lord, who as a competent works organiser was to rebuild the Morris plant for high volume production. However, after this demanding task, he fell out with the, by then, Lord Nuffield, who had refused him an 'appropriate' salary and shareholding for running the production side of the business.

An economics journalist was to say[2.2], after Lord's exit from Morris Motors 'here was a man on whom the fate of the motor industry was to rest for almost thirty years'. Leonard Lord lacked the understanding and concern for his staff as well as the design and marketing flair shown by his predecessor. He was a ruthless operator who detested 'anything approaching sophistication in running a business'. He was described as 'crude in speech and manner . . . victim of an inferiority complex . . . frequently guilty of rudeness approaching cruelty'. He later avenged himself by joining Austin and soon after becoming CEO of that company following the death of Herbert Austin. This was to have a markedly negative effect on BMC after 1952, when Austin and Morris merged, and Lord became CEO of the corporation.

Motor industry culture hung on the choice of production model

1905 had seen the setting up of Austin Motors, the first indigenous UK motor manufacturer to foresee the prospect for volume production' in the wider UK economy. By 1906 the reforming Liberal government swept to power and had Winston Churchill and Lloyd-George as innovative ministers of state, each favouring manufacturing progress. However, the Bank of England and City of London continued pushing for policies to aid the financial sector rather than the industrial interest. Even the British Fabians supported the German concept of imperialism combined with a nation organised and led by the state. But the British state, in contrast to the German one, was operating on the principle of 'muddling through' rather than significant planning, at least until World War 1, and as late as 1916. From then until 1918 much was done under Prime Minister Lloyd-George's leadership to revive the British industrial machine, for the 'war effort', including the formation of 218 national factories, albeit equipped with foreign machinery.

The concept of 'production models' came about with the increase in mechanisation of manufacturing production in the 19th century; they were used to differentiate between means of organising factory production and associated industrial environments. The clash of craft - and mass-production manufacturing techniques in the 1880s was a result of the US pioneering mass production in large corporations while the UK held on to craft production in their smaller firms, albeit organised within a factory system containing a degree of mechanisation. Initially in the UK, 'craft control was not eliminated . . . because proprietary capitalists had no organisational alternative to put in its place'[2.3]. This even applied in the newly emergent volume car-industry of the early 20th century, in that craft-like organisation of production was relying on 'craft workers to plan and co-ordinate the flow of work'.

It was argued that generally the production model in UK manufacturing involved a flexible form of production based on general-purpose machinery and skilled labour in an environment of customised demand[2.4] (*ibid.*). Indigenous UK manufacturers even in the 'new' industries initially employed a craft production model, followed by a 'craft-mass' model as the prosperity of the working classes increased, and with it increased demand for mass-produced products such as cars. Prior to that there were few economies of scale and the 'sunk-cost' technology of the production line mostly could not be afforded.

Herbert Austin's descendents pointed out that former cycle companies that converted to car manufacture at the turn of the 20th century had successfully adopted a degree of US mass-production techniques[2.5]. However those motor firms, which had spun off engineering concerns, reflected the British tendency to make the entire vehicle rather than to assemble bought-out components, the process that a number of overseas makers of the time preferred. With typical UK makers remaining dependent upon skilled workers, 'who monopolised production-knowledge', their hard-won shop-floor management techniques remained underdeveloped. While some growth in managerial power was seen during World War 1, between worker and manager 'the transfer of authority remained incomplete'.

When production-line working had been introduced at Ford-UK, weekly earnings in 1914, for semi-skilled employees, were £2.94/week compared with £1.89 in the average UK motor factory; this caused considerable industrial unrest, despite the lower wage offsetting lower productivity. Later, heavy investment in mechanisation at Austin between 1924 and 1928 led to a one-third reduction in the workforce at a time of rapidly increasing output, to improve productivity[2.6]. In terms of capital accumulation, by the 1950s, Ford's assets which in 1929 were below those of either Morris or Austin, had outstripped their combined asset value, but Morris and Ford had had comparable rates of asset growth during the 1930s despite some differences in production models.

In the United States manufacture of standardised products in high volumes, using special purpose machinery and unskilled labour, only really worked because of the size of the market in that country, the long distances between population centres and homogeneous tastes among car buyers[2.7]. The UK market was different in each of these respects and was 'dominated by quasi-luxury demand until well into the 1920s'. UK support for the part craft, part mass (craft-mass) production model for motor vehicles during the inter-war years was appropriate since even by the end of the 1930s, when demand for cars was expanding, it had not yet reached the whole of the UK middle classes, and mass-ownership of cars was not realised until the late 1950s[2.8].

Drawbacks of the fordist production model

Increasing investment in mass-production techniques was one of the key features of fordism, a labour process involving moving assembly-line production and semi-skilled labour[2.9], defined in the *Introduction*. Where a developed economy was not fordist it was still obliged to adopt a mode of growth complementary to the dominant fordist logic. As the UK economy moved over to this production model, it neither completely accepted nor rejected fordism and was to adopt flawed forms of the model. Despite the moderate growth achieved in the 1950s through mass-production methods, the UK rarely got the same returns as those obtained in competing economies. This was partly due to a productivity disparity between the US and the UK, giving rise to a slow comparative rate of UK growth, the result of the UK's distinctive form of union organisation and poor skills among UK managers. A high rate of imports was one of the consequences. Other factors which were to have negative effects included the City's place in the global economic order and industry's continual commitment to former imperial markets.

New Ways for Indigenous Manufacturing

It was claimed that successive UK governments vacillated between free-market and corporate strategies, but each time they were thwarted by lack of an ability to promote the prepared strategy[2.10]. One of the results of Taylorist scientific management (*Taylor had introduced time and motion study and related techniques to US Ford at the start of the 20th century*), a typical 'Ford-type mass production' situation, involved the removal of power from the artisan and its transferral to owners and managers. Fordist de-skilling led to an alienated workforce and a management view of former artisans as 'untrustworthy members of an opposing class'. The outcome was a domination of capital over labour alongside scientific management's objective of increasing production efficiency. Taylor had 'in total contrast to craft working . . . advocated a complete separation of conception from execution'.

Fordism in the US eventually began to develop into 'Sloanism', with the consolidation of General Motors, under the renowned CEO Alfred Sloan, whose corporation made cars for 'every purse and purpose' in four autonomous divisions serving different price bands, involving interchanging parts and more sourcing from outside[2.11]. GM overtook Ford in sales by 1927. What since then has characterised the US 'Big Four' (including Chrysler and American Motors), and subsequently 'Big Three' (after the latter two merged), was that these car-makers had powerful advertising and dealership networks to force up the cost of competition. Competitors were obliged to follow diseconomies of scale in body tooling as they strove to follow the styling trends set by the large US companies, leading to their eventual demise.

Under the embryonic but flawed fordist practices in the Manchester Ford-UK transplant established in 1911, US officials refused to let local managers develop a model (*either product - or production-*) specifically for the local market until 1928, concentrating only on cost savings from mass-production. Austin and Morris pursued a more pragmatic strategy, competing on the basis of new models and designs, as well as price, and only gradually moving to higher production volumes. Production methods were less rigid and capital-intensive, with greater customisation of bodywork, more adaptable machine-tools and greater use of labour in assembly.

However, it was felt that the comparative lack of commercial success of the UK motor industry was due to trade union power and state intervention, thus distracting from the UK 'new' industries' failure to fully adopt the fordist mass-production model, in the early 20th century. But this is refuted by those who see the full fordist model as inappropriate anyway to the UK (and since then even in the US) and thus blame institutional and economic constraints for manufacturing decline[2.12].

UK 'craft-mass' production model once preferred over Fordism

The indigenous UK production model involved product quality and continuous improvement of the production process rather than exclusively price competition, with profitability depending on introducing the right new model in an evolving market. Longer job-times were required for individual workers to achieve quality but, despite this, flow-line production was used in firms down to the size of early Humber and Rover plants. Austin and Morris had 'devised the most effective product and labour strategies to respond to the growing and shifting market', moving into volume production after World War 1, and looked for continuous improvement in the production process rather than seeking a fixed level of productivity[2.13]. They maintained flexibility by frequent product improvements and prompt response to seasonal/cyclical fluctuations by lay-offs and short time working.

The so-called craft-mass model was fully developed by the main volume builders by 1925, with substantial mechanisation in place. There followed three decades of economic success in which output increased four-fold, return on capital was consistently high and indigenous UK firms dominated export markets. Austin had 31.2% return on net capital assets from 1929 to 1938 and the productivity gap with the US narrowed for Austin and Morris, both companies distributing substantial dividends.

The superiority of fordism, in giving maximum authority to the 'new managerial class', was questioned in the light of Ford US using security police to monitor workers and Ford UK sacking union members[2.14]. Until 1932 UK makers departed from the fordist approach by accounting for consumer preferences on vehicle-performance, running costs and comfort rather than just on price. They only 'selected those elements of fordism which seemed useful for flexible production policies' and thus chose not to invest in completely automatic transfer machines that required long production runs, nor machine-pacing that required large standardised throughput. They thus opted for flexibility offered by a low level of integration and purchased parts from very well organised specialist suppliers at keen prices, thus exploiting external economies of scale.

William Morris (later Lord Nuffield) did indeed prosper for a long period with a production model which had some aspects of fordism but also had a policy of outside-purchase of major running-unit sub-assemblies such as engines and drive-train systems. Yet with arguably greater long-term success, his rival Herbert Austin had prospered with the alternative approach of a vertically integrated plant, initially retaining a substantial skilled workforce and adopting a production model peculiar to the UK involving both craft and mass production.

This was in tandem with the plant making most running-unit sub-assemblies in-house, and indeed using skilled personnel to build dedicated machine-tools in-house, in order to mechanize production. Parts that were required from outside came at keen prices from an established UK engineering industry that had embraced automotive component manufacture. These suppliers benefited both from the Austin and Morris operations, and later from other indigenous manufacturers that came into volume-production. The parts and sub-systems manufacturers increasingly specialized and gained in expertise, eventually enjoying scale-economies by serving both indigenous and transplant vehicle-makers.

Alongside the problems about forcing fordism on to the indigenous UK motor industry, and the lack of the necessary national economic support, the deskilling of workforces in the industry, which accompanied moves towards mass production, caused very considerable friction between owner-managers and skilled craftsmen[2.15]. Both had substantially contributed to the organization of production at 'shop-floor' level in the earlier stages of the motor industry. The difficult labour relations climate arising from the social conditions prevailing in the UK also meant that this friction created considerable bitterness in the workforce, which almost certainly prejudiced UK labour-relations in later years, and dampened enthusiasm for fordism. Indigenous makers, Austin and Morris, felt unable to choose full fordism and found the hybrid craft/mass model more appropriate to their more slender capital bases, though Morris was closer to fordism at Ford UK than Austin in respect of assembling fully-built running-units bought from outside suppliers.

From the early part of the century mistrust between management and labour also obviated against full fordism, as there was effectively an absence of any management control over the workforce. There was also the problem that the association for car manufacturers (SMMT) represented both the building and distribution sides of the industry, leading to different agendas for the manufacturers, and the mercantile interests of dealers. It was also argued that UK makers, in accounting for consumer preferences on performance, running-cost and comfort, rather than just price, was in contrast to the original model of fordism.

A number of employers declared that piecework had been part of their strategy for gaining control over new production systems, and that day-rate payments common to fordism were unsuitable. The argument[2.16] that only the pure fordist model could render the degree of capital accumulation required for sustaining businesses also seemed doubtful in view of the relative success initially, when compared with Ford and GM Vauxhall, of the indigenous companies in capital accumulation. This is shown in *Table 2 of Appendix D* (the low retention by Austin was a special case following its near liquidation in 1921, due to government postwar policy, and subsequent cost of servicing refinance capital. Return-on-capital figures due to Maxcy and Silberston (1959), shown in *Table 3 of Appendix D*, also suggest reasonable return on capital by the indigenous makers compared with Ford.

Shortage of investment capital

By the turn of the 20th century the economic situation had also worsened dramatically due to lack of export trade, with world commodity prices falling by one-third in the last quarter of the 19th century[2.17]. That period had also seen the further advancement of the mercantile interest with the amount of overseas investment increasing at the expense of that available to manufacturers from the new industries; this was as a result of a vast increase in the size of the British Empire during that time.

When the Macmillan Committee was set up in 1931, under the guidance of Maynard Keynes, it reported a serious gap in provision of long-term finance for smaller companies below the threshold of a stock-market issue, banks seeing it as a job for investment banks, which hardly existed at that time. In Barclays' case lending to small businesses was non-existent excepting for 'dead certs'[2.18].

There was still a high proportion of investment in traditional manufacturing industry derived solely from profits of individual companies[2.19]. And the 'new' industries were contributing only a small percentage to GDP at the time of the first census of production in 1907. It was believed that the 'root of the matter . . . was a failure in innovation and development, widespread and deep-rooted in the British economy (of both finance and manufacturing sectors)'. The individualism displayed by managers in the earlier staple industries was inappropriate for the new industries, where cohesive management was required[2.20].

Despite Lloyd George's vigorous defence of manufacturing, after 1906 a major constitutional crisis seriously delayed the enactment of government policy: between 1906 and 1914 the House of Lords opposed social reform measures passed by the large-majority Liberal government, and this was only curtailed by royal intervention. Meanwhile, by 1907 some 1170 trade unions with 2.37 million members, considerably influenced by revolutionary socialists, threatened industrial stability[2.21]. By 1918 Labour staked its claim to being the main opposition party and class politics had arrived with a vengeance. Slaughter of men during World-War 1, and the slowness of demobilisation afterwards led to further industrial unrest, exacerbated by the communist revolution in Russia in 1917[2.22]. In 1921 eighty-five million UK man-days were lost in strikes and unemployment also soared in the slump of that year.

While the UK continued to discount the ability and talent of the majority of its population[2.23], with unfortunate consequences for future economic growth, the US offered opportunities for advancement and social mobility for its people, with derivative advantages to its industry. Even in Germany's 'class-ordered society' rigorous specialist training was given to those selected to advance in the industrial hierarchy. Meanwhile, at Manchester's Trafford Park industrial estate by 1933 some 300 US transplants had arrived, establishing a period of increasing foreign direct investment that was to dramatically weaken the market prospects for indigenous manufacturers in coming decades.

Fears of globalisation and FDI

Trollope's *The Way We Live Now* had already given a good description of earlier aspects of globalisation and the sort of financier who came into being after the first submarine telegraph had been laid, between the UK and USA, to revolutionise the speed of trans-Atlantic transactions[2.24]. One of the major factors from 1914 onwards, however, was to evade tariff barriers, as Britain was ceasing to be a free-trade country with countries beyond its empire. There was also the opportunity with FDI for foreign countries to take advantage of British imperial preference and thus gain access to markets in the prosperous dominions.

By World-War 1 the switch from a Liberal free-trade to a growing Conservative and Unionist 'tariff-reform' policy encouraged overseas

MNEs to set up transplant operations in Britain for vehicle and light engineering goods manufacture[2.25]. The US Ford company for instance was quick to take up this opportunity, in the particular case of the car manufacturing sector. But Ford had a tremendous advantage in a massive homogenized US home-market that enabled them to build in-house running-unit assemblies with considerable economy. By initially establishing its UK plant as largely an assembly operation, it was able to achieve very low prices for its cars by importing these low-cost sub-assemblies and concentrating on a single vehicle model for which it had already built up manufacturing experience in the US.

Ford's final UK success was delayed for almost two decades, however, because it was selling into a differentiated market which had limited purchasing demand in the mass sector. Until the early 1930s the car market was confined to middle and upper class buyers with highly customized demands, at first relatively successfully met by indigenous makers and importers. This was despite the severe set-backs experienced by indigenous makers during World War 1, while American companies took over UK export markets and suffered relatively little cost to their home-market production.

Its Dagenham plant opened in 1932, and enjoyed competitive small car models, designed and developed in the US for the UK market. The UK stock-market had no compunction in financing much of the project and the largely Conservative-dominated UK governments of the 1930s freely assisted the operation. Then, alongside the Ford transplant, General Motors (GM) had bought-out the once indigenous-car maker Vauxhall and formed a transplant that introduced the Opel Cadet model from its sister transplant in Germany. The joint effect on sales was dramatic, with Austin and Morris losing a substantial amount of its UK market share during the 1930s, to Ford and GM.

New Ways for Indigenous Manufacturing

The earlier opening of the Ford plant in Manchester had a major effect on the indigenous motor industry, particularly as World War I had seen a great advance in the US parent's production and sales in its home territory, while UK civilian-vehicle production was largely halted by the war[2.26]. One negative effect was the importation of what was an unwelcome industrial culture for local manufacturers. For example, Ford had tried to gain further productivity advantage at its Trafford Park plant in 1924 by closing down the Sports and Social Club. It also introduced an exclusive franchise dealer system which was quite contrary to contemporary British practice; as well as losing staff goodwill the company also lost a large number of distributors.

American direct investment in European manufacturing was not just as a manifestation of technological superiority in mass-production but also partly as a means of obtaining local currency for purchase of raw materials from developing countries with which Europe historically traded[2.27]. Some countries have regarded the harmful effects of foreign control as an offset, preferring to allow the transfer (of expertise) to take place by other means, such as purchase of patented techniques and improved training. It was the motor industry, the most important in the US economy in the inter-war years (employing 4.3 million people by 1937), that particularly enjoyed this competitive advantage in its manufacturing base. It was also closely interwoven with the Canadian auto-industry and the North American share of world auto-trade was said to have grown from 25% to 79% between 1913 and 1923.

A more enlightened approach to growing a motor industry was perhaps shown by Japan, who subsidised its own producers to offset the scale effects of its overseas competitors in the 1920s and had government policy designed to encourage 'the development of a purely Japanese motor industry, gradually choking off the American subsidiaries (operating in Japan) once they had outlived their usefulness' . . . 'multinational companies were not allowed to remain once they had transferred their technologies'. Thus the Japanese state has played an important role in protecting the home market to permit business organisations to develop and utilise their productive resources, to the point where they could attain international competitive advantage[2.28]. This approach promoted co-operative R&D, given access to inexpensive finance and provided industry with a highly educated labour force to fill blue-collar, while-collar and managerial positions.

Near revolution in the labour market and growth of financial sector

UK firms were at a disadvantage in that across all industries, by 1914, amalgamations had brought larger aggregate production units, both in free-trade England and protectionist US, France and Germany[2.29]. Organised monopolistic production gave the stimulus for union-organised labour, both unions and employers having striven to limit competition, the former by demarcation agreements. This was confirmed when almost 63 million man-days were lost in strikes from 1911 to 1913. Employers' combines included not merely national trades but extended to foreign concerns, making free trade 'of little or no effect'. With the rapid communications available to combines, even free-trade Britain was finding it hard to compete against the internationally-linked combines making treaties between themselves.

The late-Victorian experience had bred rentier attitudes in politicians, resembling those of the 18th century Dutch state, noted for its pioneer banking activities[2.30]. Not until after World War 2 was Britain 'to shake out of this . . . attitude, towards the job of putting the national workshop and sales system in order'. On the labour front after World War 1 mutinies at demobilization in 1918 set the tone for the hostility, violence and disorder which characterized the years of peace to come[2.31]. Short-lived feverish booms and endemic depression in the basic industries revived all the aggressive traditions in labour disputes experienced in the pre-war years. Violence after 1926 gave way to apathy only when all the main organized political parties had failed to overcome the problems of unemployment.

UK dispensers of capital were not alert to the prospects of modern technology, unlike those in Germany, and investment was steered towards fixed-income securities and overseas ventures, the latter raising the price of capital for the home market[2.32]. After World War 1 prices had risen dramatically due to the massive expenditure incurred in waging war. Revolutionary fever was in the air and a UK Communist Party had formed in 1920 and post-World War I distrust between management and labour delayed the establishment of managerial-control of industry[2.33]. Although there was strong growth of the new industries in the latter part of the 1920s, the world slump of the early 1930s caused UK unemployment to rise to 3 million (15%) while Imperial Preference, formalised in 1932, resulted in half UK exports between 1935 and 1939 going to empire markets, away from the keenly competitive markets elsewhere, and invisible earnings were severely depressed.

The debacle in the 1920s, when Churchill was persuaded by the financial elite to rejoin the Gold Standard at pre-World War 1 parity, was devastating for both sides of industry since the pound was over-valued by 20% and many markets were lost[2.34]. After World-War 1, it became more evident that the pervading business culture was that of comparative advantage in commerce and finance rather than in manufacturing[2.35]. At the same time cultural partnership between directors and 'practical men' in manufacturing management had both parties still distrusting theory-based knowledge, while the provincial industrial elite generally were becoming subordinate to a new Conservative-based national elite.

Decline of the industrial middle classes hampered management

The period up to World War 2 saw social class and status aggravating the attitudes of industrial workers, while merchants and service-industry entrepreneurs had come to represent a major part of the elite classes, as the industrial middle class withered[2.36]. The renowned UK cultural historian and novelist, George Orwell, insisted that the unskilled working population was still formed by its 'feudal rural past', and a clinging to the out-of-date and inefficient, while an irrational support for the 'two-nation' society was shown by the intelligentsia[2.37].

The division of the upper-class elites into the London-based financial and the 'landed', from the rural counties, was weakened by a diminishing influence of the latter between the wars. The institutions of the old Establishment still flourished, albeit drawing in more outsiders[2.38]. The aloof superiority of London/South-Eastern mercantile elites increased the growth of their political, social and economic power in the capital, as the power of the industrial elite in the provinces further weakened and eroded.

The decline of Liberalism had undermined a major source of middle-class power in the provinces, strengthened by a migration of the better-off, including industrialists, from town to country. Industrial managers earned considerably less than their professional counterparts, and top earners remained those who processed rather than created wealth[2.39]. The two-class society became politicised between Tory and Labour and the children of the elites continued to be drawn away from industry by the culture of the public schools and ancient universities, but this was leavened by the advance of the provincial universities. Even Prime Minister Baldwin projected a pseudo-ruralism, during each of his terms of office between the wars, despite his coming from an iron-working family[2.40].

Recruitment problems for industry arose as a result of the anti-capitalist attacks by Labour, also the condescending attitudes of civil servants, professionals and writers[2.41]. The new super-rich from finance and business increasingly bought its way into the aristocracy, and George Orwell was to note that the UK was 'the most class-ridden nation under the sun'. World-War 1 had driven away any trust the common man had in the ruling class and popular newspapers such as the influential *Daily Mail* prejudiced the outlook of their readers, which Arnold Toynbee had suggested was the 'polluting of any enlightenment that might otherwise have flowed from popular education'[2.42]. By 1939 the total circulation of newspapers reached 10.6 million and most of them were charged with 'reinforcing opposition, particularly among the middle class, to progressive change'[2.43].

Adverse effects of industrial protectionism

Protectionism expanded during the inter-war period with 60% of British manufacturing subject to cartel agreements. Mergers were of the type that allowed private companies to enjoy short-term monopoly power but without long-term benefit of integrated shared resources. While many merged corporations were structured as multi-divisional enterprises on the US pattern, this was noticeably less so in Germany. By the late 1930s the demands on UK foreign currency stocks, arising from overseas industrial investments by the financial sector, became a semi-permanent source of balance-of-payments difficulties, on capital account, as the manufacturing contribution to trade balance also declined[2.44]. Motor industry productivity had improved substantially but was offset by depressed exports arising from the rise in interest rates. This rise, which resulted from the UK coming off the Gold Standard in 1932 and the effect of the currency devaluation in the US and Japan, in turn increased the cost of capital to industry

By the later 1920s, despite the difficulties, the new industries were becoming competitive with overseas rivals and by 1938 the UK was the world's top exporter of cars. However, this was with the proviso that a number of makers were by then foreign transplants, and questions were asked about the quality of management in indigenous enterprises, cushioned by empire markets, and lack of long-term capital investment that encouraged 'repair and replace' over 'root and branch re-equipping'[2.45]. Small rising manufacturing firms in the provinces had difficulty obtaining any capital from the stock exchange and in this respect were at a great disadvantage compared with French and German equivalents. The emergent motor industry in particular had been affected by earlier over-investment in railways that delayed the construction of roads suitable for motor vehicles. Railway development had also benefited from the 'gifted mechanic' and 'practical man', who were later a burden on the motor industry having little systematic technological education during their work experience.

From 1915 the new industries (*including transplants*) had been effectively protected by the McKenna duties (*imposed in World War 1 on luxury goods, including cars, and retained post-war in the UK)*[2.46], the effects of which were shown up by the brief experiment in free trade in 1925 when imports in those industries jumped up from 15 to 28%. The tariff was quickly restored and continued up until the mid-1940s, and its effect extended by general import duties applied after the 1931 recession, plus the effects of Imperial Preference. In 1937 imports were less than six percent of sales and for the UK car industry some 97% of sales were going to protected markets. In the case of home sales a considerable share was taken up by middle-class buyers, the price of a car being equivalent to that of a semi-detached house in the provinces.

In 1937 just 47% of the working population was in manufacturing, while service industry employment had risen to 36%; there was also appalling waste of productive capacity as skilled workers at the quality end of the labour market were unable to find employment[2.47]. The re-armament programme from 1936 was beyond the capacity of UK manufacture and excessive imports resulted. In addition, despite the many innovations from UK scientific research, industry had failed to develop them commercially. Even by 1939 cars sold in the UK were only four per thousand of the population, as a result of low income levels.

By the onset of World-War 2 a 'second war' had broken out between the UK Cabinet Office Economic Section and the Treasury, the former looking for industrial advance and the latter clinging to 'the fiscal constitution of the 19th century'. However, the government still managed to move towards a planned economy during the war and a surprising co-operation with industry was achieved.

CHAPTER 3

Industrial/national culture, 1945-1975 relative decline of indigenous UK manufacturing

Historic absence of appropriate education for manufacturing staff

Even by the outbreak of World War 1, Barnett[3.0] maintained that there was a nonsensical myth that Britain had better engineers and businessmen than its rivals when in truth many early industries were run by 'ill-educated men'. Faith in the 'practical-man-managers, who had learned on the job during and after the Industrial Revolution, had been 'based on a fallacious reading of events'. This cult of the practical man led to a distrust of the application of intellectual study or scientific research to industrial problems. In much of mainland Europe, by contrast, the state rather than being absent from such initiatives was instead modernised and made efficient, with the notion that the national interest should come in front of private profit.

'Little of the late nineteenth century scientific progress, intellectual speculation, colossal industrial developments and social change, penetrated the public schools'. Their typical products up to the 1930s had suffered from the 'greatest regimentation, stuffiest self-satisfaction and conformity, and most torpid intellectual life . . . dooming the variety, spontaneity and open-mindedness that had hitherto been the saving grace of the British upper classes'. It was also emphasised that there was physical separation of upper-class children, at preparatory and public schools, from the world in which they graduated and would eventually have to make their way. The teaching staff of the schools was equally withdrawn from the world, being mostly ex-public-school boys who had passed on to the 'equally sheltered cloisters of Oxford and Cambridge', and thence back to school'.

Despite the British motor industry eventually becoming the largest in Europe between the wars its indigenous leaders were also basically 'practical men', with William Morris a bicycle maker educated at his village school, William Rootes and Herbert Austin former apprentices, but in Austin's case a talented designer. It had no resort to graduate engineers or managers, in-house R&D or professional design departments. Meanwhile, unlike the situation after World War 1 when the Ministry of Munitions was abandoned, after World War II a new state-sponsored military-industrial complex was formed, 'devouring the best of the nation's limited resources in *Technik* and managerial talent'.

Post World-War-II motor industry recovery: fast and then slow

Under influence of the mercantile interests of the City of London, the Labour government had urged merger on Austin and Nuffield with the aim of obtaining greater economy of scale and the 'advantages' of other aspects of fordism. But similar pre-war interests had fostered imperial preference in the UK economy, which had guided the motor industry away from the more competitive export-markets, principally in mainland Europe, for which motor companies would have had to upgrade their range of models.

Herbert Austin's death in 1941, and Lord Nuffield's general withdrawal from key production and product planning decisions at Morris Motors, and his interference with the decisions of his second-in-command, Miles Thomas, all meant that unprofessional managers were generally in charge at both leading indigenous companies. Nuffield had by then neither the commitment nor the leadership required for driving the group forward: alternating between neglectfulness and inappropriate intrusiveness. The remaining 'practical-man' cultured managers at Austin and Morris plumped for car-models with traditional styling, and conservative product-engineering, models which were to become outsold by the product engineering of Volkswagen, and by the styling of US cars.

Lord Nuffield's approach to man-management largely consisted of telling people about the shortcomings of their colleagues. There was a 'distressing climate of suspicion and indecision' and there was only spasmodic strategic thinking. Management structure had changed little since the 1920s and there was a distinct abrasiveness in labour relations. By the 1940s lord Nuffield, had had a seminal disagreement with his talented managing director, later Sir Miles Thomas, who had challenged him over his gross interference with the policy-making decisions of his senior executives, despite Nuffield having relinquished executive responsibility; this was combined with an otherwise absentee chairmanship during frequent globe-trotting. With Thomas resigning, the by then 'Nuffield Group' fell behind Austin Motors and were to become the junior, if not the least vociferous partner in the eventual BMC merger of 1952.

By 1950 Lord Nuffield, in his relatively advanced years, had become chairman of the Nuffield Group, with the earlier Morris acquisition of Wolseley and Riley plus the incorporation of MG. However, both Nuffield Group and Austin Motors profited well from the dire post-war shortage of cars; but there was substantial competition from UK-owned Hillman (by then joined in the Rootes Group by Singer), and from Standard Motors (soon to be partnered with CV maker Leyland). Even setting aside the gradual increase of imported vehicles from mainland Europe, there was also substantial competition from the two US transplants, making up the British 'big six' motor-vehicle makers, Ford and General Motors (comprising in the UK both Vauxhall Cars and Bedford Trucks). By the end of the 1970s Ford and GM transplants together were to overtake the indigenous volume manufacturers in market share.

Although Austin and Nuffield had been encouraged by government to amalgamate in the belief that economies of scale would allow them better to deal with the competition from rivals; such amalgamation had cultural implications. The first post-World-War 2 decade was seen as the time of a tragically missed opportunity for the restructuring of the indigenous UK motor industry; that contrasted with the manner of that performed by Japanese industry's controlling body, MITI[3.1].

Clouds gather over the nascent British Motor Corporation

By 1952 Austin and Nuffield, as the merged BMC, were weak in models for both home and export markets in certain car-size categories. However, pent-up wartime demand had kept them busy up until the time of the merger. The merged BMC then faced expanded operations at Ford and GM's transplants by the end of the 1950s, as well as opposition from US Chrysler that had taken over Rootes

Motors in the UK. Within BMC, senior managers remained too faithful to their formerly independent Austin and Morris concerns, and failed properly to integrate operations. The new corporation was thus faced both with dispersed factories *and* contrasting management ideologies. The British Motor Corporation was doomed by the inability of the two differently cultured firms to co-operate effectively and properly to reap the scale advantages of the combine.

Throughout industry many mergers had no complementary advantage to companies and the stock exchange ensured any resistance from targeted firms was undermined: half the listed UK companies disappeared between 1957 and 1969[3.2]. There were modest taxes on capital gains compared with those for profits and dividends, which increased the popularity of share-exchange take-overs. However, within seven years of merger, profits made by merged companies were usually below those of the separate companies in the three year period before the merger.

After the British Motor Corporation merger, CEO Leonard Lord presided over the dismissal in September 1952 of seven hundred workers, including seven shop stewards, at the Longbridge works[3.3]. It was a response to the National Union of Vehicle Builders after their strike at Austin in March of that year, which had been the largest single-firm stoppage for the UK motor industry. Wider effects of industrial mergers were also being felt: for example the 1952 BMC merger resulted, by 1956, in a further 6000 reduction in the 55,000 workforce without any management discussion with employees. This was at a time when competition was becoming fiercer in the European market; yet when a strike was called, following the announcement, only 50% of the workforce responded.

In contrast competitive mainland European car-makers were noted for co-operation between management and labour during industrial disputes, a far cry from the UK situation[3,4.] One researcher said it was then mainly UK labour-relations that was holding back industry, citing the political philosopher GDH Cole who claimed that 'centralisation of collective bargaining has done a good deal to encourage the belief among (union) leaders that they own the members, rather than are owned by them'. The answer he felt was in fostering free activity at branch level; this was also a time when liberal thinkers were advising plant-level bargaining for wage norms rather than at national level.

Misguided actions of BMC directors

At BMC, CEO Leonard Lord's deputy, George Harriman was to comment that Lord had 'set back the full integration of the two companies (Austin and Morris) by a decade' and a former BMC executive claimed that Lord failed to deal with complex legal arrangements between the marque-dealer networks and the corporation, thus for seven years preventing the company from reducing the number of body-shell types produced[3,5]. The corporation's retail dealers persuaded BMC into an arrangement whereby they could recall advance deposits made for new cars if the corporation failed to meet rapid availability after a launch. This however required cooperation from the unions, which was not forthcoming, since Lord had not brought them into an atmosphere of mutual trust in the early stages. It had caused problems that would probably have been avoided by the paternalistic Lord Austin. Meanwhile, BMC had been held back by weak marketing and lack of attention to fleet and export markets.

Design Director Issigonis failed even to acknowledge faults on cars until serious customer disaffection had built up, it was argued. He then became pedantic when asked to sanction restorative changes.

New Ways for Indigenous Manufacturing

He and his fellow directors would not countenance the employment of university-trained graduate engineers who could 'improve and refine motor vehicles' so as to avoid such detail design faults, using sophisticated design prediction techniques and development-testing to obviate the need for the customer to be plagued by in-service faults. Single-minded Issigonis was bewitched by the success of his revolutionary design for the Mini and 1100/1300 models but was stubborn in reproducing the innovative drive layout for the larger Maxi and 1800 models for which it was thought to be unsuited. BMC's design director turned down an innovative 1.5 litre rear-engine car (designed to rival Citroen's DS19), developed by engineering consultants ERA, for BMC[3.6], as an alternative to his front-wheel drive transverse-engine formula for these *larger* cars, which were not really outstandingly successful in sales terms

The autocracy of both Leonard Lord and Alec Issigonis was to prove an unstable mix in the British Motor Corporation (BMC), when compared with the totally different approach to manufacture by the constituent founders Herbert Austin and William Morris. Lord at BMC was pressured by the mercantile interests of the marque dealers to retain distinguishing body designs (and thus marque identities) for different models and hence into prohibitively costly production facilities for the most expensive part of the car, its body. Dealers were too short-sighted to recognize that they were not primarily competing with one another's marques, within BMC, but with those of the big three US transplants in the UK while Alex Issigonis's eyes seemed totally closed to the production-engineering and operational-reliability aspects of his designs.

Marketing failures even included announcing new car models ahead of production, thus generating long waiting lists and customer frustration. Model renewal cycles were also much longer than those of the US-owned transplants. Even twenty years after the first merger the Austin and Morris dealer networks were not rationalised. Despite the popular launch in 1959 of the Mini model, sales success had been restricted by annoying faults in detail-design.

Growing competition from the transplants

Even in the late 1940s potential output of Ford's Dagenham plant was a million vehicles per year, way beyond the 700,000 maximum of BMC (*op. cit., 3.2*), which barely reached minimum economy of scale by 1952. With GM's 1920s takeover of Vauxhall, and Chrysler's takeover of Rootes by the late 1950s, this put huge pressure on indigenous makers. These big transplant players could segment the market into size categories and enter each segment with one of its model-categories, while BMC's limited number of model-categories, as opposed to individual models, could only compete in a narrow band of market segments. Another disadvantage of overseas transplants lay in the relationship of the transplant with the national government. The UK government's steel allocation policy during the Korean War of the 1950s had favoured Ford, who had an option to withdraw from the market at any time, and so like other US concerns were able to ignore government advice on price controls and profits, while UK firms were forced to co-operate under the threat of nationalisation.

The medium-size car sector of the UK market was dominated by Ford's Cortina (and later GM's Cavalier) while BMC lacked the appropriate model for that lucrative sector. The Marina model intended for that role came later, under BLMC, and was not a success, while the competing Ford Cortina was also designed for the fleet market and the 'up-and-coming' prosperous worker appearing on the 1960s scene, not least those employed by the Dagenham Ford

Motor Co and its associates in Essex. The car was considered to have 'sex-appeal' and attracted an enormous new market.

The late 1940s saw a massive expansion of Ford UK and by 1948 graduates were recruited and trained by the company, at a time when top management at Ford US was replaced by Henry Ford II's protegees[3.7]. 1951 was the year of the opening of the massive Port Talbot steel strip-mill destined to feed the, by then, booming UK car industry with sheet steel. Sadly it was also a time when Austin's Longbridge plant was strikebound, involving ten thousand workers under the guidance of 350 shop stewards, 50 of whom had Communist sympathies, but who were mainly shouted down by fellow workers at strike meetings.

Meanwhile, GM-Vauxhall by 1949 had gained 11% of the UK car market. Its main models were given Chevrolet-style makeovers in 1951 and a smaller, largely US-styled, Victor model was to follow in the mid-1950s, cashing in on the Americanisation of much of British national,culture. GM was to undertake a huge expansion of the Vauxhall transplant by 1956 (*graduate recruitment had already started there in 1954*). It was said of GM that 'only a firm backed by a giant industrial grouping could have afforded to embark upon such a large investment programme over such a short time period', indicating the immense advantage of US transplants over indigenous makers[3.8].

It was surprising to some that even in 1950 the whole British motor industry had enjoyed 52% of worldwide motor exports. But since 1948 the UK Ford transplant had been both the highest volume, as well as the most profitable, maker and by 1950 its production over four years had trebled. However, Ford's overly inflexible, macho approach to management that had worked in the unemployment-scarred 1930s was less suited to the relatively full-employment post-war era. Up to 1949 there had been 40 strikes and go-slows in three years. 'It seems as often as not to have been a tough-mindedness that, counter-productively, allowed an insufficient degree of dignity to the workforce'. One Ford worker has been quoted:

> *"those of us who worked in the Dagenham plant recall the fear of talking out of turn, leading to suspensions and even worse if one spoke out. The Gestapo-like Service Men wrought fear in the workforce, and the cat walk high above the factory, where the superintendent usually patrolled, made him 'for all the world' like a prison warder.*

About that time another Ford, Dagenham, car worker had commented on working conditions at his plant:

> *It's got no really good points. It's just convenient. It's got no interest. You couldn't "take the job home". There's nothing to take. You just forget it. I don't want promotion at all. I've not got that approach to the job . . . . It's different for them in the office. They're part of Ford's. We're not, we're just working here, we're numbers'.*

This 'instrumental' attitude of many workers had serious implications for the long-term health of British industry, the workers' political vote going to the party that 'came up with the goods'.

A recent assessment of BMC's comparative market 'failure'

The conventional view that the collapse of BMC/BLMC was due almost entirely to trade union irresponsibility has been long challenged by Steven Tolliday of Harvard University[3.9], who carefully examined prime causes attributable to UK government and corporation management. He also reminds us that an alternative opinion, of other researchers, was that prior to the 1970s the industry had been too slow to take on the Fordist mass-production technology and production-management system. He points out, too, that despite this suggested failure the indigenous volume producers in the late 1940s retained a fairly steady forty percent of the UK market; the same was being held by BMC after 1952 despite the commanding presence of transplant operations by US giants, Ford since 1911 and GM since 1925.

BMC was operating in a fast expanding UK market, but it was one of mainly affordable small (and low profit margin) 'mini'-cars in the 1950s, and super-mini cars such as the BMC 1100-1300 series in the 1960s. Both such car size categories were the same cost, or even more, than larger size ones to build. Because of the national diversity in demand no manufacturer in the UK was able to gain more than fifteen percent of the market, and this usually from an assemblage of a variety of models each selling in small volumes. With the introduction of the BMC Mini in 1959 the continuing labour intensive methods meant that no single operation on the production line was less than 144 seconds compared with the 40-60 seconds for their US transplant rivals and little automated equipment was available, so productivity was low at 7-9 cars per man-year.

Performance of BMC relative to transplant manufacturers

Leonard Lord's neglecting of the fleet market for BMC cars was a grave mistake, in that it was effectively subsidised by tax allowance *(op. cit. 3.7)*. Most of Lord's executives had worked their way up from apprenticeships, their long rise to the top 'deluding them into thinking they knew all aspects of the business and its markets'. The firm's craft-mass production model gradually became inflexible, with its associated autocratic paternalism, plus the expensive accommodation made with the workers.

From 1957 to 1962 UK makers (indigenous and transplants) enjoyed a quarter share of the world's car market; thereafter the share shrank to one fifth and the later decline of the industry was heralded, with the recovery of continental manufacturers[3.10]. In 1955 four cars per year were made by a single British industrial worker compared with five cars in Germany, soon rising to eight, a situation arising from Britain lacking economies of scale on key competing car models.

This was compounded by the structural industrial-relations problems which BMC's head, Leonard Lord, blamed it all on shop stewards wrongly characterised by the popular media as being exclusively communist sympathisers. This was at a time when top-level representation in the management of companies was given to shop-stewards with the proviso that interruption to production were minimised. Meanwhile UK governments of the period were still devoted to foreign 'inward investment - whether or not that investment would undermine Britain's own indigenous industry - (and) successive British governments went out of their way to help foreign multinationals such as Ford'.

By 1956, in her remarkable turn-around since 1945, Germany succeeded the UK as Europe's largest car producer, with BMC overtaken by VW. By the 1960s, Ford UK was acquired by the US parent and enjoyed a massive expansion with £526 million spent on plant and equipment, a capital injection that was to defeat indigenous makers in the following years[3.11]. Rootes by then had surrendered to Chrysler, with generous grants from the UK government. The UK car market was considered to have become homogenous by 1963, with the increase in hire-purchase buying, but enforced relocation of firms by the government was an economic setback for the industry.

It had been argued *(op. cit.3.2)* that BMC had reacted to government persuasion by expanding car production from 300,000 units in 1952 to one million per year in 1965. The home market absorbed this by expanding to six times its former size but exports rose by just less than one third in the same period and by the end of this time markets across Europe began to become saturated, at one car per 3-4 people. The small Mini and larger 1100/1300 models took 25% of the home market in peak years of the 1960s and other specialists models were introduced by the corporation to obtain a total share of 40%, but competition was fierce from Ford and GM-Vauxhall with their Escort and Viva models in the smaller car sector.

Growth in globalisation a further threat for UK's ability to innovate

Globalisation began to take off after World War 2 and the massive expansion of American firms by overseas investment led to a rapid increase in transplants in the UK and elsewhere in the early post-war period[3.12]. British official statistics on FDI only began in the early 1960s and Dunning's work (*American Investment in British Manufacturing Industry*, 1958) is cited as the best record prior to that time.

By the mid-1960s American firms accounted for a significant share of UK national production. It is pointed out that even in the advanced economies American firms produced 75% of the computers sold in Europe, and an even larger proportion of integrated circuits for the electronics industry. Non-American companies were by then seeing a world dominated by American capital, and being forced to accept a subordinate role in growth industries such as electronics.

Yet ironically, a former senior partner of McKinsey and Co, said that Silicon Valley, the engine of the US microelectronics industry, had become notably protectionist, creating industry associations, establishing a polished lobbying presence in Washington and discouraging (even barring) foreign investment, let alone foreign takeovers[3.13]. It is sometimes suggested that US acquisitions in the UK are offset by those of the UK in the US. However, according to researchers, apart from scale differences, UK overseas acquisitions resulted in abnormal negative returns for 1991-1996, giving support for the notion that companies would have been better served by promoting growth from within[3.14].

Criticism of the impact of foreign multinationals on host countries has been that they often reserved managerial and skilled jobs for home-country nationals 'thereby limiting the spin-off benefits of improved managerial techniques'[3.15]. It was also 'far from axiomatic that foreign transplants introduced superior technologies . . . nor did the motor-car industry have substantial examples of technology transfer. Ford remained dependent on its American parent in matters of design', while indigenous makers Austin and Morris had instead benefited by importing production machinery direct from America. 'Few American firms in Britain decided to join employers organizations because this meant recognising trade unions . . . Ford and Pressed Steel (had) held out against recognition until 1944'.

In the UK generally, indigenous manufacturing was particularly vulnerable to foreign MNEs, which preferred to locate in high-income markets rather than in places of less expensive labour (in 1975 41% of FDI took place in the USA, Canada, the UK or Germany). The UK had been a preferred first location in Europe of the pioneer American multinationals, and two hundred of them were surveyed in the UK during the 1950s when the beneficial effects of the 'competitive and dynamic qualities' transferred from US to UK economies were noted[3.16]. However, reports of superiority of US transplants over UK indigenous manufacturers have to be treated with caution, especially where the production model does not well match local factors of production. A subsequent survey that covered 685 foreign parent companies with 927 UK manufacturing subsidiaries found that US FDI value in British manufacturing had risen from $542 million in 1950 to $1,611 million in 1959, and reached $2,521 million in 1962, in one of the fastest growth periods.

UK governments were accelerating the decline of emerging indigenous vehicle manufacturing concerns by giving an unfair advantage to the established US transplants: by treating American companies in Britain equally with British-owned companies, successive governments permitted unrestricted inflows of foreign capital, which were detrimental to the competitive position of the indigenous industry. UK attractiveness for foreign direct investors during the 1930s could largely be attributed to the fact that Britain then had the highest per capita income in Europe, a high population density, excellent transport and the bonus, for Americans, of a common language[3.17]. British finance was even used to set up France's Renault and Citroen manufacturing subsidiaries in the UK.

While a comparatively small *number* of foreign-owned companies entered motor vehicle production before 1962, this dramatically understated their overall importance to the British economy. By 1962 foreign companies accounted for a quarter of total British employment in the vehicle sector, and nearly one-third of the sales, while vehicle manufacture accounted for almost one-fifth of total foreign owned assets in Britain. In 1962 three US companies, Ford, Standard Telephone & Cables (STC) and GM Vauxhall, employed around one-fifth of the workforce employed by foreign-owned companies in British manufacturing, with 61,000, 32,000 and 24,879 workers respectively.

Throughout this period British governments put almost no restriction on foreign takeovers of British companies, and this highly liberal policy undoubtedly further increased the attractiveness of Britain as a host economy. Inward investment represented 7.2 per cent of the British GDP in 1967, compared with the 3.2 percent average for developed market economies as a whole. This made inward FDI much more important in Britain than in other large European economies such as Germany, where it was 1.9 per cent of GDP, or in the United States, where the figure was a telling 1.2 per cent.

Prosperity led to change in the national culture

Political attitudes generally in the 1950s were increasingly affected by the improved economic outlook, with raw material prices falling and the start of the 'golden age' for the industrial West3.18. But it was also the start of a time of voracious company take-over operators in a City of London unused to contested acquisitions. The take-over marked the end of the long tradition of family capitalism in the UK, and provoked severe disapproval in the trade-union movement and elsewhere.

It was also the case that, corresponding to the state of the business cycle, company taxation was varied six times throughout the 1950s while purchase tax and excise duty were altered nine times, and credit control changed eleven times, the latter causing serious dislocation to the industries involved. In the 1950 s and 1960s affluent Britain was becoming both a 'consumer society' marked by the huge increases spent on advertising, and a 'permissive society'.

The considerable spending power of the younger generation that had developed, alongside the further adoption of American culture, was accompanied by disillusionment with a class system that had remained intact even after two periods of 'socialist' government

During the thirteen years of Conservative rule from 1951 to 1964 there was both full employment and a record increase in productivity in this so-called 'golden age' for British industry. Car population rose from 2.5 to 8 million and the average wage from £8.6s to £20.6s, but Britain was 'inefficient in its materialism, with slow economic growth compared with other competitive nations'[3.19]. Short-term gains in income were substituted for long-term growth, exacerbated by a voting system that would have led to change in government with a very small swing in the popular vote, and an electorate expecting annual increase in its income.

Towards the final indigenous UK volume motor industry merger

Relentless external pressure on BMC to progress towards fordism urged the company on to an annual output potential approaching, but not achieving, a target of one million cars per year. The lower figure was the result of either too many body designs being made as a result of manufacturing economies; or perhaps in the inability to compete strongly in any one market sector. Loss of market share continued until 1968 when the next merger was urged upon the company. Another member of the pre-war 'big-six', Standard Motors, had already merged with Triumph and the then profitable commercial-vehicle group Leyland had become Leyland Motor Holdings (LMH).

It then seemed rational to the government that BMC and LMH should merge to form BLMC. But all these mergers were ill-conceived given the unwillingness of the separate managements to co-operate. Fordism, again urged on the industry by government, appeared also to be the wrong course to take for the UK industry which had a home-market nowhere near the size of that of the US and one still a good way off the homogeneity of this, the largest, competitor nation. The merged companies, having gradually lost their independence, were also much less incentivised to develop profitable niche markets.

Meanwhile, US transplants in the UK, by then having their expansion programmes part-subsidized by the government, were able to fill all UK market segments with appropriate models and volumes. The UK 'indigenous champion', BLMC, was only able to compete in a very few of such market segments and was handicapped by ex LMH senior managers, who were unused to high volume car production, by this time the corporation approaching one million vehicles/year production rate. BLMC was unable to bring suitable competitor models to such diverse market segments.

Widespread prosperity eventually brought greater homogeneity to the market, which by then succumbed to the styling of the massively promoted products of the US transplants. Meanwhile BLMC managers, under pressure from some of its formerly Ford-employed managers, and the UK government, urging a fordist approach, did not take the opportunity to adapt the hybrid 'craft-mass' production model, to bring it closer to the emerging Japanese flexible-specialization model, which might have enabled it better to promote its diverse model range for specific niche sectors of the market.

Originally, with a market share initially of 35%, BMC had been described not as a merger but a take-over of Morris by Austin (with HQ at Longbridge), having as CEO Leonard Lord who was hostile to Morris directors in the group. It was 1958 before the first corporate car model, the A40 Farina, was announced and only by 1960 was a record profit of £26.9 million achieved (Ford's profit was £33 million for building 182,000 cars less in that year). By the time of the British Leyland Motor Corporation (BLMC) merger in 1968 home market share was just 28%. Rootes and Standard's share was about 10% each[3.20].

BLMC had been formed by the relatively small commercial vehicle (CV) builder Leyland, with its car-making subsidiaries, uniting as the *senior* partner, with the much *larger* BMC in 1968. Under CEO Donald Stokes and deputy, ex-Ford director John Barber, much of the management of the corporation was actually drawn from the *smaller* partner, Leyland. Barber, and fellow executive recruits came from the rival Ford Motor Co. This group urged the Fordism production model on to the BLMC volume car division, possibly at the expense of contributing to the five million man-hours lost in strikes in 1969.

By 1975 the poor financial performance of the volume car divisions had driven BLMC to bankruptcy and the government's Central Policy Review Staff (CPRS) were briefed to examine the situation. But the CPRS also favoured a fordist solution to the corporation's financial problems and sought to keep it in business initially by subsidies and then by competing head-on with international volume builders. Eventually BLMC was substantially restructured by the new CEO Michael Edwardes appointed in the late 1970s, when a medium volume production capacity was agreed upon, and a respected restructuring programme nearly completed.

Prior to that, the priorities of the stock market, of providing the option of short-term liquidity for shareholders, had led to undercapitalisation of the corporation *(op. cit. 3.8)*. Though 45%

capture of the car market was forecast, only 35% was achieved and the management style was that of a personal enterprise, lacking the necessary injection of professional organisation and control.

Motor industry managements were still an unhappy mix of 'upwardly-mobile members of the merchant-class and downwardly-mobile members of the (aristocratic) rentier-class'. Meanwhile British top-executives seemed more attracted by 'machinations in the money markets than in building up stable manufacturing concerns'[3.21]. An increasing trend in industrial culture was that invoked by that extreme fragmentation of work and rationalised production of standard products that partly characterised the fordist mass production model, which was urged upon the indigenous industry[3.22].

Workers were not members of a clearly defined work group or 'trade' and were controlled by time schedules and production rates, with little personal control over their own tasks and little sense of their making a contribution. Yet despite this, at a minority of enterprises, marked improvements in performance had been noticed with *changes in management*. However, corporations such as BMC and BLMC were characterised by larger financially-struggling firms joining with smaller financially-secure companies, without appreciating that the management of the smaller firm ill-suited the caretaking of the larger firm. In 1968 productivity was only five cars per employee per week in the UK compared with twelve cars per employee in Japan[3.23] *(op. cit. 3.1)*

Later, in their car divisions, net trade balance from the UK reached £1.3 billion for the Ford and GM transplants in 1983[3.24]. This made it harder for, by then BL, to generate sales sufficient to support scale economies required to compete effectively in the UK market. This was especially so with the US MNE's transplant assemblers in

Germany and Spain exporting cars to the UK that were perceived as quaui-British. By 1991, in manufacturing as a whole, 13% of workers were employed by transplants, and even as early as the 1980s seventy percent of corporate profits in the UK were generated by MNEs, most of which were foreign parented.

Both governments, and senior industry officials, had forced mass production on companies 'regardless of strengths and capabilities'. The 'practical men' in BLMC management were 'amateurs unable to adapt to the changes in market demand (and) advancing production technology'[3.25]. Even heads of the two major Austin and Morris plants (at Longbridge and Cowley) were barely on speaking terms and shared few common systems and approaches[3.26]. No notice was taken of how continental competitors produced their cars and even by 1975, the year of BLMC's bankruptcy, the National Enterprise Board was to find that hardly any change had been made in the inherited BMC industrial culture years since the BLMC merger in 1968.

In marketing terms, a fatal choice had been the design of the Marina medium-size car model (the key model in the battle with Ford's Cortina), based on the running-gear of the Morris Minor and with an unstylish body, insufficiently roomy interior and engine variants trying to compete in both small and medium car sectors, together with marketing limited to the Morris dealer franchise[3.27]. A group of directors did try to instigate updated versions of the successful 1100/1300 model for the purpose but this move was overruled by Barber. By the 1980s the Marina model was even considerably outsold by the later-introduced Metro and Maestro models. The situation was worsened by the BLMC head-office working to Fordist principles, while the operating-companies, producing the different vehicle-marques, continued with the craft-mass production model.

The latter did, however, have the advantage of a low 'profitable-break-even' points at 10,000 to 30,000 vehicles/year and there was considerable flexibility in design of vehicles. The multi-divisional form of organisation which proved dysfunctional was instituted too early on at BLMC and made worse by Donald Stokes (with over 20 directors reporting to him) involving himself in the minutiae of the operation in the manner of the ageing Lord Nuffield before him[3.28] *(op. cit. 3.25)*. Both Stokes and Barber lacked direct knowledge of car manufacture in the craft-mass model, and many of their executives had little management training. Information was passed by telephone and no records were thus kept for future analysis.

The archivist of the British Motor Industry Heritage Trust, argues that the Morris Marina of 1971 was seen as 'an uninspired knee-jerk response to the double challenge of Ford's Escort and Cortina models, rather than the result of the company's own evaluation of market trends'[3.29]. Fig. 5 in Appendix C shows the output of main indigenous and transplant motor makers, indicating the timing and degree to which Ford was overtaking Austin and Morris.

Learning from the lead up to BLMC bankruptcy

Between the 1968 BLMC merger and 1974, out of total profits by the corporation of just over £70 million, almost all had been paid out in dividends, with retained capital being negligible. By 1975 a staggering loss of £76 million had been recorded, after which time the government's Ryder committee were guiding the fortunes of the nationalised firm[3.30]. Chrysler's former Rootes plants also met near collapse in the mid-1970s, attributed both to the inheritance of misfortunes from former UK owners and the 'introduction of American management techniques, which in many ways were unsuited to the traditions of industrial relations in Britain'. Also Chrysler did not have the vast funds available to support Rootes, which GM had to carry Vauxhall through these difficult times for the economy.

Another threat to motor industry productivity, at a time of rising employment in the sector, was lack of capital investment, which was 30% down on continental competitors by 1975, and even by 1972 BLMC home market share had dropped to 33%, in retreat from US transplants[3.31]. Fig. 6 in Appendix C shows Ford and GM-Vauxhall's production overtaking that of the indigenous volume producers in 1981/2, despite the run down in transplant production brought about by increasing captive imports from their continental partners towards the end of the period.

A further threat was the scale of internal industrial warfare across the whole sector, evident in 26% of total production (450,000 cars) being lost in 1974. Increasingly aggressive US-style management across the sector was one of the causes, made worse in the BLMC case by few managers understanding the details of production, and few foremen commanding respect[3.32]. However, from 1971 piecework wage payment at BLMC was gradually replaced by measured day work, for which the foremen suddenly became key line managers, which was necessary to ensure the scheduled throughput. In the event though, poor productivity was primarily blamed on the failure of foremen to meet targets.

Should trade-unions be blamed for the BLMC collapse?

After the formation of BLMC, Tolliday (*op. cit. 3.9*) suggests by the 1970s the market's first time buyers were on the decrease and fleet sales on the increase, which dramatically favoured Ford's Cortina model and BLMC models were spurned by individual drivers within the fleets who were moving towards the US culture of favouring larger cars. BLMC directors tragically failed to recognise the importance of the fleet market which had risen from seven to forty percent of new car registrations between 1964 and 1974, opening up opportunities to the US transplants in the UK that were already introducing new models that suited the American culture spreading in the UK

The Ford Cortina could not be beaten by the more cautiously designed BLMC Marina, which was further challenged by the GM-Vauxhall Cavalier, a yet larger car that even challenged the Cortina replacement, the less successful Sierra. The Austin-Rover Montego came too late in the day to challenge any of these models, exacerbated by the lack of fleet-car dealers in Austin-Rovers distribution network. Meanwhile BLMC's small cars were increasingly challenged by continental imports, cars that were also relatively unchallenged on mainland Europe because of BLMCs inadequate dealers in that territory.

The final nail in the marketing coffin was to come in the form of tied imports into the UK from Ford and GM's continental transplants. BLMCs hastily introduced, and undercapitalised development of, Allegro and Maestro models was apparently unpopular with the corporation's core customers and led to drastic loss in market share to continental imports. With the prevailing mercantile culture of UK business, the corporation was forced over the years to continue distributing profits to shareholders so as to retain their confidence and stave off takeovers. Out of £74million net profits between 1958 and 1974 for BMC and BLMC £70million were distributed.

The £2billion investment programme agreed after the 1974 nationalisation of BLMC was not allied to a clear strategic plan to restore sales, and plants fell below 60% of their full capacity.

However, up until 1978, despite the fall in market share, the share of indigenous output in the UK actually held up, and the US transplants were failing to hold up against third-party imports; only their own tied imports protected their 'British' market share.

According to Tolliday, in the 1960s union shop-stewards had actually taken on the role of chasing up supplies to the production line and persuading management into better stock-control. A late-1960s enquiry at the Cowley plant had revealed that more time was lost in shortage of supplies and machine breakdown than in labour disputes. Larger strikes were usually associated with recessions, so reduced the stocks of unsold cars, and were not a severe problem until 1968. But the new measured-day-work payment system was to encourage the occurrence of over-manning as unions no longer reduced worker deployment to keep up piece-work payments; it also had the unfortunate effect of being introduced without production-managers being retrained to optimise the new system and it took ten years to match the system with restructured work organisation.

Post World War 2 economic realities

Following World-War 2 the UK was forced by the US to run down its exports to a level below that which it was obliged to import, because it was required to prohibit currency reserves falling below a level dictated by the US[3.33]. The UK was also prevented from changing exchange-rates, so as to protect employment against deflationary pressures. Keynes's enforced committal to an Anglo-American military partnership, too, was disastrous, with the cost of UK military expenditure rising by £1.5 billion from 1945-1948.

The outward flow of British capital had resumed on a vast scale after 1945, despite the import of US capital as its transplants increased in the UK[3.34]. The City strove to make sterling attractive to foreign speculators rather than revisiting its earlier role of financing business, and the pound was thus over-valued and so damaging to industrial exports. By 1964 the British standard of living was already resting on debt, and was therefore vulnerable to the 1960s credit restrictions, which had significant adverse implications for industry, particularly the motor industry.

The 50-year interest-bearing loan from the US, following Lend-Lease, put the UK under US economic control, and ended imperial preference, with the City forcing the pound to be kept at a high value and the government obliged to use stop-go measures damaging to industry[3.35]. Capital investment per worker fell considerably below that of foreign competitors[3.36]; while another researcher maintained that the pervasive mercantile culture induced manufacturers to try making profit from take-over rather than from improving productivity and marketing[3.37].

Cultural effects on decline of the indigenous UK motor industry

Britain was seen as having made an error of judgement in embracing the aggressive American model of management rather than those of mainland Europe or Japan, with British employees having no mechanism with which to bring any influence to bear. The fordism production-model forced on the UK indigenous volume-production motor manufactuers could only be adopted in a flawed form due to the lack of necessary background economic conditions that were needed to sustain it.

Links between the industry and academia remained impaired, while industry-academic bonds were strong in Germany, and breadth of knowledge was also greater among German technology graduates entering industry. It was considered likely that UK opinion-leaders in politics, education and the civil service were affected by the anti-industrial attitude prominent in UK culture. The crippling effect had been to draw the 'ablest products of our society' away from UK industry. It has been suggested that our manufacturing rival Germany had an overlaid culture of hard work relating to job-satisfaction rather than of merely earning money; such a culture put competing by superior design/manufacture ahead of buying market share by company acquisition.

Industrial culture was also influenced by political culture and political parties were no longer divided on strictly caste lines as a new post-World War 2 plutocracy of super-rich bankers, financiers and businessmen bought their way into the traditional aristocracy; the industrial elite effectively becoming subservient in an economy increasingly dominated by the financial sector. Meanwhile a kind of 'personal' management had developed in the indigenous motor industry in which individual executives of holding companies involved themselves in both operational *and* strategic decision making. Normally industrial leaders convinced themselves that they had no need to bring in well trained managers from elsewhere.

Workers on the other hand suffered from a deep class-consciousness, as was revealed in a 1960s study of mostly motor industry employees, mentioned above. Almost in the manner of the upper class, they appeared to belong to primitive 'estates' in which they were not in fact seeking out 'social' improvement. It was argued that overseas societies had class related to function but in the UK the battle between upper-class power and organized union power meant continuous hostility to middle-class efforts in smaller-scale industry.

New Ways for Indigenous Manufacturing

Industrial culture was also affected by national culture, which in turn was strongly affected by the amalgamation of newspapers and the disappearance of many provincial independents. As newspapers joined the ranks of 'big-business' this led to the promulgation of opinions biased towards the financial sector, and a consumer society that would benefit newspaper advertisement sales. In the broadcast media even by 1954 the BBC's radio programme *The Archers: an everyday story of country folk* reached a radio audience of ten million, tuning into a currently popular dream of 'country-life' by the general public long after most of the population had been urbanised.

The previous year was that in which commercial television had been licensed and a battle for viewers had commenced with BBC television. This further limited the range of broadcast opinion due to the general dumbing-down of the content of both broadcasters, despite some isolated cultural highlights. By 1979 Thatcher had welcomed in a 'homogenised Americanism' that encouraged the heritage trade and service-consumerism, which was largely divorced from manufacturing.

An economic culture damaging to industrial reorganisation

The three year Korean War programme was to cost £4.7 million, at the peak in 1952/3, 12% of GNP, and involve conversion of 25% of the metal-based industries to munitions production, as well as the UK providing 22,000 men in battle. This was at a time when Standard Motors' plant in Coventry was scheduled for production of Avon jet engines required for the RAF's war programme, for which 10,000 workers would have been needed, which could have involved diverting a quarter of the 1950 labour force engaged in civil motor car production.

The notable European sociologist Professor Ralph Dahrendorf, later of Oxford University, thought Britons lacked the urge for material achievement which drove his former German countrymen; he said that in this sense: 'Germany is middle class and Britain is not'[3.38]. Such British domestic spending that existed was mostly done with borrowed money but the German counterpart at that time was from the 'fruits of extra effort and individual saving'. British society as a whole in the late 1940s was restricted by 'convention and hierarchy'. National complacency arose from attitudes to World War 2 when Britain rejoiced from a self-imposed pat on the back for its part in the war effort: the psychology of a victor, although material circumstances resembled those of a loser.

There was a false belief that the empire was a benefit rather than a drain of resources. In the absence of a system of government like that in Germany, of strong links between the government, industrialist and trade unionists, the Labour government was faced with a civil service establishment with little ability in industrial reorganisation. While it had been decided before the war to develop technologies for the 'new industries', the facilities for making office machines and systems hardly existed, for example, and the will to restructure 'ramshackle existing industries, such as motor vehicles and computer hardware, was missing. There was no British equivalent of the French *Commissariat du Plan* for remaking Britain as an industrial society'.

National culture had affected the industrial culture

Kynaston *(op. cit. 3.18)* noted that by the end of the 1930s about a quarter of the UK population had lived in suburbia, condemned by a senior planning consultant for 'its social sterility, aesthetic emptiness, and its economic wastefulness'. Most of its estates had been constructed by speculative builders with little regard for town planning and the inmates were referred to scathingly by George Orwell in respect of their lack of ability to change UK economic fortunes. However, wartime itself had seen a new devotion to political planning in government circles, but with the foundation of several new ministries and a quarter of a million more civil servants. Maynard Keynes had finally convinced the deeply conservative Treasury of the need for demand management of the economy and in his book *The Middle Way* Harold Macmillan, in 1937 of the Tory left, had called for a programme of nationalisation as least as ambitious as that of the Labour Party.

During the World War II banks had been taken under control and government inspection of firms' books made allowable, to make intervention easy to apply, and a more disciplined regime was experienced in manufacturing[3.39]. But after the war UK decline relative to other nations had been associated in the public mind with 'end-of-empire and increasing hegemony of the US'. One notable pioneer of cultural studies[3.40] said this had led UK opinion-leaders to see fordist production as the only solution to decline'.

The economic situation had deteriorated ten years after the war; the 'election budget' following Churchill's retirement in 1955 had pushed the government into a 'stop-go' economic management damaging to industry, Kynaston *(op. cit. 3.18)* suggested. When the third election in a row had been won by the Conservatives in 1959 it was suggested that there was an 'embourgeoisment' process in which many manual workers took on the life-style of the middle classes. But this was disproved when the sociological survey *The Affluent Worker* was published following the study of Luton car workers.

A 'them-and-us' attitude was pervasive: almost an urban form of the peasant/country-house relationship of the *ancien regime*[3.41]. People thus hesitated when put forward for such roles as factory foremen; they were inhibited, too, by memories of pre-war unemployment. There was also much less self-interestedness among the wider working class than is now the case. A study, mentioned above, of affluent workers in Luton's motor and related industries showed that there was little inclination for 'turning middle class', while middle classes were becoming divided between urban and rural elements, but with some increase in the urban sector corresponding with the growth of new occupations in the technological industries.

Changing cultures of the middle and working classes

World War 2 had had a unifying effect both on UK social classes and management/labour in industry[3.42]. In the post-war British theatre's 'kitchen sink' dramas provided insight for the middle class into a working-class culture that imposed harsh pressures for conformity. Although the spread of mass culture gave the impression of greater mobility among the classes, the reality of a growing 'underclass' was often overlooked. Division of urban and rural elements of the middle class was stimulated by the so-called 'heritage industry' of looking backwards, with interest in stately homes and ancient pursuits. Multiple layers of class were identified as impeding social and industrial relations and UK capitalists were becoming averse 'to the slow grind of building up manufacturing businesses', quick returns having greater appeal within the rampant UK mercantile culture[3.43].

The emerging 'service class' became even more evident in the 1960s, with professionals and managers from the middle classes shunning the earlier entrepreneurial tradition of 'inventing and making things', the new tradition being defined by life-style-advertising that inculcated social cohesion by appealing to a long-gone past[3.44].

Probably affecting the more desperate of industrial workers, there was a considerable amount of pro-Russian sentiment, despite only two communist MPs being elected in 1945. British Communist Party membership then reached 50,000, having tripled during the war. There was also distrust of Americans who were seen as 'throwing their weight around' following the abrupt end of Lend-Lease, and MP James Callaghan condemned their 'economic aggression'. Labour's nationalisation programme had been held back by restrictive business guidelines placed upon it by politicians, including prohibiting diversification into manufacturing and no institution of any sort for worker participation in management. There were 'nationalisation boards, . . . including not just businessmen but a motley crew of peers and retired generals', as well as too much interference by government ministers.

Given the British Communist Party's near complete lack of electoral success it devoted most of its efforts to industrial disruption. The Electrical Trades Union had to put up with a Communist executive for many years. In general most unions suffered from too large a gap existing between the executive and the rank and file. Headquarters became increasingly national and remote from local centres of trouble. Despite the existence of apprenticeships in the 1950s, three-quarters of teenagers entering work found themselves in jobs without any craft or career training available. Industry was also increasingly affected by cartels, applied to 25-30% of manufacturing output and rising to 50-60% in the 1950s, with 'incredible levels of price fixing'. On the union side restrictive practices were seen as cheaper, and possibly more effective in outcome than strikes.

For the middle classes, the past became 'a refuge rather than an inspiration' and lack of consideration for ordinary people was partly attributed to glorification of the ruling class, seen in the 'media attention paid to Elizabeth II's coronation'[3.45]. A deferential society was in place, while the bourgeois culture of the industrial middle class 'was in retreat before the London-Oxford-Cambridge axis' of the elite. Luddism in intellectuals did not reflect a Britain trained for wealth creation, technologists in particular being 'sadly neglected' and/or untrained in human terms. Oxbridge became a place to 'acquire social prestige rather than confirm it', graduates often plumping for 'service' activities such as broadcasting, finance and advertising, with high income potential. Monarchy had 'defined the British not as citizens but as subjects', leading to an unhealthy conformism and snobbery; it was also the 'branding device of the heritage industry'.

In 1955 the political commentator Henry Fairlie said in the *Spectator* that UK political parties' equivalent in power over the nation, was the 'Establishment', which included not 'only the centres of official power . . . but rather the whole matrix of official and social relations within which power is exercised'. His article had significant impact and was the major post-war attempt to unpick the connections, and penetrate the secrecy, of what was still at the top a very much *closed* elite. The Treasury, too, was an institution of great prestige as well as mystique, where a secretive mandarin culture ran deep[3.46].

A former Cabinet Advisor[3.47] argued that 'Royalism . . . promoted rank, birth and money over ability . . . and the survival of a royal aristocratic elite . . . (became) an astonishing fact', while down the scale of caste 'rough and ready empiricism' was too much a guiding force for UK management. Britain's elites promulgated the idea that the national culture was anti-ideological, with any criticism of this view being dismissed as the 'ravings of the marginalised'. The carefully managed reputation for anti-intellectualism gave the idea that character training was still the true aim of UK education, 'favouring the mercantile operator who may not know much but is excellent at getting on with others'.

This public school ethic was even thought to have spread to the grammar and secondary schools. However, only the grammar schools encouraged the notion that education was a question of scholarship and learning, producing people who were notable exceptions to the UK norm, sharing some resemblances with the graduates of France's *Ecole Nationale d'Administration* who dominated her business life.

Educational constraints on industrial progress

A former headmaster of Westminster School, maintained that in WW2 there had been increasing fears that public schools would become anachronistic in post-war Britain and hence the government's setting up of the Fleming Committee to examine how they could be more closely associated with the general education system[3.48]. It reported in 1944 that public schools should be open to all who would benefit from them, regardless of parental income. But neither the LEAs nor the schools themselves put the recommended schemes into practice, the LEAs having inadequate funds for the purpose. Labour MPs themselves, often having had earlier local political experience as councillors prior to entering parliament, refused to allow the Ministry of Education to run the schemes.

When critics charged the public schools with replication of a single class in positions of professional influence, the schools argued it was the school-leavers' inculcated qualities of leadership that imbued these advantages, rather than an 'old-boys' network'. Critics quickly replied that British leadership in public service or private enterprise 'had been singularly inept when compared with the leadership in our competitor countries', where public schools were absent. This was because the public school concept of leadership excluded qualities such as imagination, vision, willingness to innovate and awareness of technological change. In many cases they 'produced loyal, reliable conformists, admirable men to police a far-flung empire but not for holding key positions in a century of rapid change'.

While grammar schools in the UK had performed excellently for twenty years after World-War 2, secondary-modern schools suffered with less well paid and less well-qualified teaching staff. Grammar schools were then being infected by the snobbery culture in the private 'public' schools, which they tended to ape, as well as being generally better resourced than secondary-moderns. By 1950 private schools were almost fully subscribed and educated 180,000 of the 5.5 million children at school.

Also nearly half the children at grammar schools were of middle class origin and their parents could presumably have afforded private education. Governments generally were not shy in making changes to maintained schools but are hesitant about independent school reform. This was followed by a period from 1973 to 1979 in which an inflationary crisis almost trebled school fees and put pressure on enrolments. By 1980 there were 2000 independent schools in the UK, 1350 recognised by the DES.

Historians now ask: 'can it be chance that Britain's long decline from the last quarter of the 19th century coincided exactly with that period in her history when the public-schools . . . were at the height of their influence'? Not only was there conformity but narrowness in a curriculum accentuating classical studies, and in life-style the schools were 'brutal, philistine societies condoning homosexuality, institutionalised sadism and the worship of games'. They were also criticised for enjoying an unfairly high staff-pupil ratio, not sending boys into industry and being disdainful of modern technology. All these criticisms provoked the Headmasters' Conference to take public-relations more seriously after the 1960s.

Although Harold Wilson's 1964 government had a clear intention of tackling the 'problem' of public schools, nothing was done and in 1974 all forms of tax relief and charitable status were put forward for removal, but again nothing happened. Labour backed away from public school reform and feebly switched to banning selective grammar schools in the maintained sector. Labour thinkers such as Crossman believed removing the grammar schools would give a new lease of life to public schools, by appealing to parents disenchanted with comprehensive schools.

Comprehensive education was by 1965 to take the less favoured form of just merging together existing secondary-modern schools and even by the end of the 1950s only 4.5% of school leavers went on to higher education and among science students only 36% were in technology, compared with 68% of German students[3.49]. Different school-leaving ages in the UK, of 15, 16 and 18, were 'loaded with class values' that were unknown in the US, so that emotional strain in parents was communicated to children.

There was often even bizarre opposition to university men making careers in industry from some management quarters in the 1950s. By 1966 23% of the new supply of scientists was leaving the country, and 42% of technologists [3.50]. Also 'the vast majority of graduates in UK industry were going into and preferring research rather than production management'.

Successive governments' failure to sustain industry

The post-World-War 2 Labour government acceded to wage demands in order to avoid disrupting production[3.51]. Trade unions were still against worker-participation in management and the prominent observer Anthony Howard had said of the 1945 Labour government that its election had 'brought about the greatest restoration of traditional social values since 1660'. With upper and working class ministers in the two main parties of government preferring large-scale organisations, little interest was shown in true private enterprise.

A former education and science minister felt a British classless society could only be achieved by the redistribution of wealth, rather than income, to remove the social hierarchy of schools and to transform the psychology of industrial relations. This would ensure that the worker received a new social status preventing his/her total exclusion from rights of participation, something that Labour had not yet offered. Chancellor Stafford Cripps, between 1947 and 1950, was one of the few politicians that had take a positive approach towards industry and to be rewarded for so doing by industrialists.

His problem was that out of twenty of the Labour Cabinet, thirteen were amateurs without industrial experience and of the seven others all but one were trade unionists. Of the senior civil servants most of their knowledge of industry was though 'reading *The Times* in the Oxbridge senior common rooms'; this went along with a first secretary of the treasury who did not pretend to know anything of economics. Meanwhile, private industry was beset by nepotism among its directors and below them managers were profoundly conservative, risk-averse and both mentally and materially unambitious.

Sir Nigel Fisher, biographer of former PM Harold Macmillan, points out that when Labour regained power in 1964, inheriting a sterling crisis from their predecessors; its attempt to inspire a technological revolution was hampered by the poor competitiveness of UK industry and a civil service comparing badly for industrial efficiency with the French technocracy[3,52]. Spiralling wages caused a defensive inflation of interest rates and some 50% of research and development (R&D) expenditure was directed towards the military, as compared with the continental average of 25%[3.53]. Stock reaction from government to poor industrial productivity was to 'consume, and invent less, rather than produce more',

During PM Harold Wilson's Labour government the newly formed Department of Economic Affairs was at loggerheads with the Treasury, so preventing industrial restructuring. High military expenditure continually threatened the balance-of-payments, which, in an 'open economy', was given more attention than was growth[3.54]. Although modernizers strove in vain for the French model of indicative planning to be set up in the UK[3.55], from 1964-1977 bids for economic growth were frustrated by incompatible targets of reducing unemployment while retaining stable prices[3.56]. Between 1959 and 1970 rapid changes in governing parties had taken place when neither could solve the problem of economic decline, and production fell in relation to competitor countries[3.57]

While there was British enthusiasm for science, little was known about how to harness this in an effective manner. Heavy UK expenditure on R&D was channelled into the new industries but this kind of research was better exploited by other countries in turning research into innovative products[3.58]. Encouragement of firms in these sectors to re-locate to areas of declining old industries weakened the competitive power of companies. Industrial relations were marked by a 'snobbish and often uninformed management entrenched on one side, with an immobile, unambitious workforce . . . on the other'. By the end of the 1970s days lost in strikes were over 13 million/ year and after the incoming 1970 Heath government, industry was 'recognisably subjected to political pressure by the trade unions, which were too readily damaging the economy and the community as a whole'.

Onward march of globilsation

As globalisation spread in the following decades FDI began to look like 'commercial colonisation' as major US corporations bought rival companies, to reach monopoly position, market share being 'purchased' rather than 'won' in the traditional competitive sense[3.59]. The domination of foreign MNEs in the UK was indicated by the fact that they were responsible for 70% of corporate profits by the early 1980s. There was a tendency, too, for foreign MNEs to use the UK merely for assembly operations, and the product and process technology brought in was 'intermediate' between that of lagging UK firms and that of leading MNEs. The main cause for concern was that technological dependence on foreign firms had led to a 'downward spiral in the field of technological innovation', and its exploitation in the UK. However, labour militancy in transplants was said to be less intense, due to the threat of production being relocated to another country[3.59].

From 1945 to 1965 the number of US firms setting up in the UK had been likened to an 'invasion' and the value of US FDI in the UK grew from $542 million to $2521 million from 1950 to 1962[60]. Even as early as 1931 40% of US-owned plants based in Europe had been located in Britain, and in the late 1940s UK exchange controls thwarted the US goals of multilateral trade. Initially UK policy was designed to curtail the short-term dollar drain, but in the longer term the intention was to overcome the continued payments imbalance by encouraging US firms to establish subsidiaries in the UK.

It was also suggested, across all sectors, that indigenous industry was investing a great deal of its own manufacturing resource into a given product area but the inward investor was often merely an assembler and not therefore competing on equal terms. Foreign firms might also make little use of indigenous suppliers and may not create a large number of higher skill jobs. Withdrawal of transplants could lead to diminishing of the local education/training infrastructure in a way that could make start-up of new indigenous enterprises more difficult. The setting up of transplants often tended to absorb new indigenous start-ups and the FDI presence could thus make further development of indigenous start-up enterprise impossible. Foreign direct investors usually had the benefits of a large home capital base and the main beneficiaries were usually the capital raisers in the country of origin.

Generally the priority of transplants in mature economies was monopolising market share, their presence making industrial restructuring from the political centre difficult to implement. Later it was found that US automotive MNEs supplied 'captive imports' from their continental transplants through a dealer network seen by government and customers as quasi-British. Increase in assembly of imported car kits from Ford and GM's mainland European operations combined with captive imports of completed vehicles were eventually to reduce local parts/labour content. Finally it was found that, in terms of value-added and employment, one assembled car kit from Japan had been less valuable than one British manufactured car' (50% local content compared with 80-90%).

Nation-states no longer have power to compete, in industrial terms with a continental-scale economy (*op. cit .3.60*). States tend to act in their own perceived interests, with the UK deliberately seeking to attract FDI through her recent relatively low-wage economy, also following the strategy of exporting capital to earn higher returns and relying on foreign firms to do its industrial investment. The effect has been to convert the UK into a branch-plant economy but the UK has actually been described as an 'over-internationalised country in an under-globalized world'. These 'outpost' transplants could result in fairly mindless assembly work and standardised management systems, with less demanding work on the shop-floor and less original work for technologists. Historical experience had shown that the UK workforce responded better to the challenge of difficult skills, personal responsibility and intellectual demands.

By 1994 25% of UK GDP was produced by imports from foreign firms, even without the substantial slice produced by foreign transplants operating in the UK. In that year the UK manufacturing economy had slipped to 11th place in Europe, and Europe itself lagged behind Japan and the US.

CHAPTER 4

Decline of indigenous UK manufacturing, 1975-2005

A malign cultural inheritance

From the end of World War II the British establishment succumbed to the myth that Britain was a world power with resources to match, rather than face the reality that the empire was more of a liability than an asset in economic terms[4.0]. With notable exceptions Britain's industrial culture was effectively still stuck fast in the relatively primitive stage at the end of the Industrial Revolution, a period when the unique nature of supremacy she had then won had bred arrogance and self-satisfaction. Meanwhile, in America and on mainland Europe, it had been the state which provided the basis of the required professionalism via complete national education and training schemes: primary, secondary, vocational and technical.

Prime Minister Atlee had presented one of his most penetrating papers to the Cabinet Defence Committee, which carefully tackled the fundamental problem shirked by all pre-war UK governments in the 20th century, that of getting British politico-military commitments and British resources into proper proportion. It was bitterly attacked by Foreign Secretary Ernest Bevin whose calamitous espousal of Britain's 'world role' throughout his tenure had destroyed the prospects of recovery for the country's industrial machine. Even post-war the motor industry itself, while willing to co-operate with the government over export quotas, also refused to countenance a radical structural alteration of its organisation.

British 'practical man' was recognised as being the very opposite of the educated practical man who was to emerge to challenge him from American and mainland European technical schools. Technical ignorance existed at all levels of British Industry and that elementary education provided for those becoming workmen or foremen was insufficient for providing any basis for further scientific study. The British educational system was not geared to vocational areas such as management and enterprise. In other countries (e.g. France and Germany) they clearly understand that they must develop industrial expertise at multi-discipline academies.

The CPRS enquiry at the time of the 1975 BLMC nationalisation, following the corporation's bankruptcy, determined that under-investment and bad work practices had been the main cause of its bankruptcy, but any resolution of this problem was made impossible by almost total insularity between the government agencies and the company-officials involved[4.1]. By then, cash margins on sales were just 6.6% for BL, compared with 10.8 for Toyota and 15.3% for GM-Opel, despite UK labour costs being 75% those in Germany[4.2]. Productivity in terms of vehicles per employee in 1973 was UK 5.1, Germany 7.3, US 14.9 and Japan 12.2., not surprising for the UK where production-line stoppages meant only 50% full-capacity utilisation.

The long-time analyst of UK business culture, Will Hutton explained that with the big-four banks refusing to take part in the scheme, this had compared very badly with Japan's rescue of Mazda, with long-term investment banks in Japan actively engaged in Mazda's successful transformation. The reasons for Mazda cars, made by Toyo Kogyo, still being a potent force in world car manufacture, while BL no longer exists, have been traced to difference in the underlying national business cultures of the two countries[4.3]. Crisis struck for BL in the UK during 1973, when production and debt servicing costs rose sharply at the same time as vehicle sales were falling. An expensive investment programme was necessary for BL to stay afloat but, in 1974, the big-four banks refused to supply the $1.2 billion required. This was on the grounds that the stock of debt was equal to the prevailing value of the company's equity, signalling other investors also to withdraw funds and the shares to drop yet again. This demonstrated the classic attitude of the UK financial system to disengage, maximise liquidity and show no long-term commitment.

It was argued that British banks knew of BL's investment plans only days before the formal request for funds was made, while in Japan, in return for financial support, Sumitomo Bank installed its own management team at Mazda. At the time when Mazda's future was threatened, the bank helped to execute a massive cost-saving programme while investing in a new model range. Even the bank's MD joined the motor manufacturer as executive vice president, a move described as 'unthinkable in Britain, despite the major banks' television rhetoric of avuncular support for creativity'.

Mazda's shareholders took dividend cuts and directors took pay cuts while managers had their pay frozen and production workers accepted pay rises below the going rate. There were 10,000 job losses, and a freeze on hiring, but compulsory redundancies were minimised by redeployment of people in the distribution network, which needed expanding drastically. The bank increased its share of the $1.5 billion total debt to 16% and sought new funds from other investors, particularly the long-term investment banks such as Industrial Bank of Japan and Long-term Credit Bank, of which no such equivalents existed in Britain.

BLMC had not reined in bought-out costs by using Japanese-style co-operation with suppliers, instead imposing price freezes and switching suppliers, and later BL was criticised for installing automation systems dedicated to just one car model rather than for multi-purpose operation[4.4]. Since there was no British equivalent to the Japanese industrial investment banks, it would have been totally against the prevailing UK financial culture for top banking executives to play active roles on the boards of UK industrial companies. They were active enough with assisting in the buying and selling of companies but the restructuring of companies to improve production efficiencies was outside their perceived remit. Meanwhile the US transplants had several advantages over BLMC; while production had been running down in BLMC's Standard-Triumph car operations in Coventry, the Rootes Group that had become Chrysler Talbot in 1967. That company received a substantial UK government grant during the Chrysler take-over, while Ford also received a £30 million grant from the government towards its new engine plant in South Wales.

Effective directorship squandered by government's aid withdrawal

The turn-around in BLMC/BL only came with the appointment of Michael Edwardes as CEO, and the gradual reversal of his predecessor's corporate centralism, plus introduction of the long-needed separation of line and staff functions in management, marked by the change in the name from BLMC to BL[4.6]. There was reshuffling of top jobs to ensure appropriate directors had a full knowledge of volume-car production and that their managers received full business training, which had not previously been the case. Product planning and cost accounting were also given more focus and in-depth psychological interviewing was carried out on all key managers prior to reorganising their functions.

Major restructuring at BL in 1977 included a de-centralisation of car production operations and better exploitation of the potential capacity of the works (which was by then producing 1.2 million units/year), together with a reduction in costs of £200 million/year. But outside pressures were more difficult to handle in the short term and these included a blatantly negative media, a crisis of confidence among dealers, tighter trading conditions, projected exchange-rate movements and a resulting fall in market share. However, Edwardes saw as his major challenge tackling the problem of militant shop-stewards: a drawn-out task only accomplished when he convinced employees that just 160 of their number were militants (the media had worsened matters by attributing militancy to the whole BL workforce). The cost of facing down the militants was some 110,000 vehicles in 1978, accounting for £200 million in lost sales.

The Conservative election victory in 1979 did not bring the hoped-for stability at BL because of the accelerating effect on the strength of the pound made exports much more difficult. 'The impact this made on BL was fundamental. It brought us to our knees', Edwardes maintained. The government were using interest rates as a lever to retain a high pound and BL's plan to earn £1bn./year from exports was thwarted, and a flood of imports resulted. Nevertheless by 1982 BL productivity had risen to over 25 cars/man-year from 17 in 1981. The first of the CEO's new car models, the small Metro, was launched in 1980; fifty robots were employed in its body fabrication, and it proved a top seller in home and continental markets.

However, the product-introduction gap, between it and the forthcoming larger Maestro and Montego models, had to be filled with a modified Honda Ballade (*badged 'Triumph Acclaim'*) heralding the international joint venture (IJV) with the Japanese maker. By the time the BL Montego got to market later in the 1980s GM Vauxhall's Cavalier model was in a dominant position, supported by German design and manufacturing teams plus US capital. The market was thus split 3-ways by its major producers and single model shares inevitably shrank; the Chrysler Avenger model also threatened BL sales and Edwardes railed against the government for not letting Rootes 'go to the wall' prior to the state-aided Chrysler acquisition.

During his stewardship of BL, Edwardes had faced continuous threats of premature privatisation of the corporation from the Thatcher government. He accused the UK civil service of undue innocence compared with their French and Japanese counterparts, for not negotiating fairer trade in terms of obtaining reciprocal access to countries whose car-makers had access to the UK. Spain, where Ford cars were manufactured in transplants, only had to pay a 4.4% import duty into the UK while Britain had to pay 36% for Spanish entry. Edwardes boldly tackled local-government property taxes (rates) on UK makers, when BL was in 1981 paying £25mn./ year, and he took legal action to prevent threatened increases of 30-40%. Captive imports by transplants were another target, with Ford having a £164 million balance-of-payments deficit in 1981, contrasting with BL which had 97% of its exports made in the UK.

After he had left the corporation, Edwardes' final complaint was against the Thatcher government for breaking up BL in 1985-6 and the premature privatisation of its volume-car division (by then Rover Group) sold to B.Ae., at far less than its true value. Including regional aid and tax breaks, the latter company's 'net gain was £397 million'. Edwardes was to accuse the Thatcher government of being 'relieved to wash its hands of the troubled firm by pushing it into the private sector' and hastening to bring in Japanese transplants. He considered that 'ideology' had been allowed to overcome 'commercial sense': perhaps justifiably when the restructured company had not been given time to meet the long-term targets. The UK government's withdrawing of financial support, at that stage of restructuring when a return to profitability was in sight, was ill-considered and seems to have been clear evidence of political opportunism. The government wanted to abdicate responsibility for BL regardless of the consequences.

BLMC/BL production increased while UK market share dropped

By 1980 the UK had fallen to eighth in road vehicle production and fifth as an exporter and over half the home market was captured by foreign imports/transplants[4.7]. Yet between 1968 and 1979, Vauxhall and Chrysler/Talbot had been below economic volumes of scale while BL, despite its troubles, maintained half of the UK output of cars, with the US transplants no more successful than BL in meeting the import challenge[4.8]. These foreign MNEs only scored in their ability to bolster their 'poor' performance with captive imports from their continental subsidiaries. Such imports for 1979 were Ford 236,824, Peugeot/Talbot 108,354 and Vauxhall 44,822 compared to BL's 16,751 from its Belgium subsidiary.

That BL, in fact, came to export more cars than the three US MNEs put together in the two main overseas markets, Europe and America, at least suggested the preference in these markets for products of indigenous firms over those of foreign multi-nationals. BLMC's pre-tax profit at £51.3 million for 1973 was the largest in its short history. However, lack of market success with new models such as Marina and Allegro later led to a loss of UK market share from

31.8 in that year to 19.6 percent by 1979, following the widespread talking down of the corporation and its products by the media during a period when the oil crises had seriously disrupted the market. It was also the case that the UK market would grow each time credit restraints were eliminated, and shrink when restraints rose again, even if purchase tax remained comparatively high: then rising again when easing of purchase tax occurred, the resulting stop-go policies being seriously destabilizing.

Different forms of individual 'production-models'

Between the BLMC merger in 1968 and the Rover Group of the mid 1990s, the corporation had been influenced by traditional 'production-models' such as Sloanism, Fordism and Taylorism, as observed at Ford in the UK, as well as being influenced by Japanese and German production models during their association with Honda and BMW. These were the indigenous 'craft-British', 'craft-mass' and 'mass-British' (flawed Fordism) models that were falling out of use[4.9].

For the earlier BMC, the mass-British model could not manage high enough output to enjoy scale efficiency while, for BLMC, adaptations of it incorporating the 'mass-British' model failed to bring commercial success; the flawed Fordist production model having been forced upon the corporation both by government and ex-Ford executives who had been recruited. The surviving craft model in the specialist car divisions allowed break-even points at 10,000-30,000 vehicles per year and gave flexibility in product design. The full-blown 'mass' model was never fully rationalised because vehicles were being produced at dozens of separate sites and although work groups were working more efficiently they refused to share the gains with the individual companies concerned, leading to serious over-manning.

The government's encouragement of the Fordist manufacturing model in the UK might well have worsened the growth of industrial bureaucracy and led to a diminished work satisfaction for both production-workers and executive staff, as had occurred in the US[4.10]. Before 1979 'flawed Fordism' (an incomplete production model) had been both 'weak on industrial investment and economic modernisation'[4.11]. With this flawed model indigenous makers did not get the same return on mass-production techniques as foreign-owned multi-nationals.

The switch to 'flawed Fordism' also created labour problems in the displacement of skilled workers in the UK. Yet BLMC, was having to negotiate with 36 craft unions, made worse by two-tier (countywide and plant) levels of wage-bargaining[4.12]. The pro-Fordism analysis of industrial decline was also questioned in the light of relatively successful service/process industries in the UK without such a production-model[4.13]. It was also argued that the multi-divisional structures of US Sloanism reaped few rewards for UK corporations and by the 1970s corporate doubt on Fordism was even expressed in the US, in the face of 'flexible specialisation' at their hosted transplants, a production model pioneered in Japan described earlier.

Rover Group privatisation soon led to the BMW takeover

Until the BMW take-over BAe's lack of long-term commitment to Rover had been obvious for some time, while BMW's purchase of Rover had allowed the new parent company to widen its product range at a time of heavy competition from US/Japan. In contrast, under the privatisation beneficiary, BAe, investment had been less than $200 mn./year prior to the takeover whereas BMW promised $450 million. On the 25th January 1994 BMW paid £800 million to B.Ae for Rover Group[4.14], despite Honda earlier having offered to raise its Rover shareholding from 20% to 47.5%, with British Aerospace (BAe) holding the same (47.5%) share. But Honda had previously charged Rover heavily for running-unit, 'chassis', assemblies and took a royalty on each car sold. Moreover BMW had allowed BAe to make a complete withdrawal from its vehicle business, bought in 1988, that helped BAe recover from its near fatal financial crisis of the early 1990s.

The directorship of B.Ae had damaged the remaining British volume builder of motor cars as had the Thatcher government's policy in its ill-considered disposal of BL into the private sector, with its rechristening as Rover Group. The value of the extensive restructuring of BL by Michael Edwardes had been severely compromised, as the corporation became a 'political football' and was demonised by the newspaper and magazine press.

Intensification of the British mercantile and deferential cultures

In the 1980s the pervading mercantile culture led to numerous acquisitions of UK firms by foreign businesses, during a period of de-industrialisation, and led to the disappearance of many manufacturing companies. Meanwhile, media coverage of royal events had in one sense a socially unifying effect, but in another sense continued to reaffirm the class divide in people's minds and the heritage industry perpetuated the physical presence of the country houses of the rural elite. The German anglophile Ralph Dahrendorf was cited as having said that he 'finds few things more bewildering than the extent to which current public debate is pre-occupied with yesterday's world'. On the ambitions and abilities of the English to run large industrial organisations, including the ill-fated car companies, the respected cultural historian Anthony Sampson[4.15] had said that firms continued to suffer from their traditional class divisions, which provided over-confident amateurs at the top, with a lingering dislike of trade and commerce, separated from the professional managers and technicians further down. It also could be said that Britain generally had made the mistake of embracing an aggressive American model of management, rather than those of the other Europeans or the Japanese.

A nice comment was made on the Conservative attitude to industry subsidies; the marked difference in government treatment of the manufacturing and agricultural industries had been observed: there were large variations in subsidies, tariffs and taxation, depending on economic sector, before and during the Thatcher years. William Keegan (*The Guardian*, 2.2.1984) pointed out that if, like agriculture, BL had had a protective tariff of 100% to keep out key competitor imports, paid no rates, no VAT, virtually no mainstream taxes and the Government agreed to buy all the vehicles it could not sell abroad, at an inflated price, then anyone could have made the firm profitable! To make matters worse Chancellor Lawson pitched his 1984 budget strongly in favour of the service sector to the detriment of manufacturing industry. The latter lost out on tax allowances for plant, machinery, stock relief, buildings and other items, compared with the labour-intensive service sector, typically trebling the tax bill for manufacturers.

The wrong focus on manufacturing within education and training

One of the principal problems of manufacturing was to overcome the reluctance, of often unqualified industrialists, to seek out the trained personnel needed[4.16]. In 1985 it was found that one-fifth of so-called managers had no qualifications of any description and in the early 1980s many industrial training boards were closed by the Thatcher government in the belief that they interfered with free-market policies. Although high levels of R&D expenditure had existed since the 1950s, some 67% of it was directed towards defence, rather than, for example, motor manufacturing techniques.

In academic research assisting industrial technology, Britain was probably held back by the class-composition of universities being the same as it had been in the 1920s. Thus some of the brightest contingent of school-leavers among the poorer classes would be lost to universities and rich students reading arts subjects would be predominant. Also a high proportion of university graduates were drawn into the civil service of the time, and a much smaller one into industry. At school level government initiatives to provide 'greater choice' for parents in placing their children was very much to the advantage of the middle classes over the lower income families, as was the Assisted Places scheme to subsidize fee-paying parents of children choosing independent schools.

While schools of management were extolling the value of teamwork in British industry, in the manner of the Japanese production model evident in the Nissan transplant, Margaret Thatcher was hailing the benefits of individualism and suggesting there was no such thing as 'society'. Apart from the lack of social cohesion, which was being recognised by opinion leaders, there was also a vital need for industrial cohesion among workpeople. On the other hand there was evidence to suggest that many people were unambitious, in the material sense, to become entrepreneurs, and a balance had to be found between a rediscovery of respect for 'long-term' and a questioning of existing 'quick buck' enterprise seen in the behaviour of many entrepreneurs. Thatcherism and its aftermath had also led to social instability implicit in the growing inequality of personal incomes. While the living standards of the poorest fifth of the population increased by one percent, the wealthiest one-fifth gained thirty percent. Worse still, for industry, the House of Lords Select Committee on Technology and Science in 1991 reported 'virtually no investment in manufacturing industry during the 1980s'.

Small 'c' conservatism and the two cultures in British education

While a contemporary positive view was presented, at the turn of the century, on degree-level learning by educationalists, and, on average, performance of 16-17 year olds in maths and science, the assessment failed to highlight the lack of provision of education across all achievement levels[4.17]. In training, too, the British individualist approach meant there was little proper partnership between small to medium enterprises (SMEs) and local agencies such as Chambers of Commerce, trades unions, local government and universities.

Under the German system in the largest manufacturing organisations, 12% of the workforce had a higher engineering qualification; and competition was tackled by 'better design/manufacture (which) always (came) before buying out the competitor'[4.18]. Companies collaborating with academia were also less evident in the UK than in Germany, and German manufacturers even by 1990 were said to have employed three times the number of engineering graduates used by their UK counterparts. Breadth of knowledge was also greater among German graduate engineers, with all students having to undergo courses in a balanced list of five major subjects.

The continental term 'technik' meaning 'useful arts and manufacture' had no precise equivalent in the UK, where it was confused with 'technology', meaning 'scientific study of the teaching of techniques'.

New Ways for Indigenous Manufacturing

Hence UK politicians thought that the teaching of technology would lead to solving manufacturing problems, and there was evidence of 'trained' UK engineers seeming to be uncomfortable with manufacturing processes. There was a failure of the British to accept and understand the prestige and specialisms of the French *Grande Ecole* and the German *Technische Hochschulen* that set the UK culturally apart.

In an interview with a senior executive, Graham Pink,[4.19] in a flourishing high-tech British company, it was explained that press reports at the turn of the 21st century had noted UK physics and chemistry departments at universities being closed down in places as far apart as Exeter and Newcastle. The difficulty was that educating future scientists and technologists was more expensive than educating arts graduates, so a simple-minded cost-cutting approach would see the science/technology faculties as the first victims. There was also the problem that in Germany, for example, 'engineer' is a respected title whereas in Britain the same name is used for someone who repairs the washing machine. A 'doctor' in the medical sense was respected but not someone who has obtained a doctorate in the physical sciences. While the professional institutions for the different engineering disciplines have promoted the term 'chartered engineer' for the past twenty years or so, outside the profession the term is quite meaningless. The British educational system is not, even now, geared to vocational areas such as management and enterprise.

Notions that Britons live in a country divided by two cultures often date back to the early years of the Industrial Revolution. This twin-culture situation caused skirmishes between different groups in society, exemplified by that between the Romantics and Utilitarians of the 19th Century. More recently a mid-20th century feud occurred between CP Snow and the literary critic FR Leavis at Cambridge University, at the time of the former presenting his

Reith lecture on the topic[4.20]. As both a scientist and a writer, Snow said he found himself moving between two groups, comparable in intelligence and social origin, earning about the same salaries, but not communicating at all. Scientists read very little of the defining novels, history, poetry and drama while literary intellectuals were ignorant of science and technology.

Class-divides and looking backwards hurt industrial performance

With unemployment touching 24.1% in 1975 a post-industrial society was forecast for Britain[4.21], and a 'New Right', surrounding the *Daily Telegraph* and *Spectator*, prepared for the Thatcherite revolution of 1979. The shrinking of the UK economic base had been the most significant development of the 1970s, with firms such as Rolls Royce and British Leyland having been taken into public ownership, and, by the end of the decade, unemployment had reached two million[4.22]. At the same time the culture of class was deeply wounding society with *The Observer* newspaper commenting:

> 'class is so deeply embedded in our national sub-conscious it is the poison of our lives. Not just industrial relations and politics, but our choice of districts to live in, jobs, friends - even which bar to drink in. It's a kind civil war we are perpetually fighting, wearing out our energy and emotions, our time and money. It holds back progress, destroys prosperity, (and) impedes social and working relations on every side'.

A culture of neo-liberalism had permeated the whole of UK society by 1989. Old forms of solidarity had been replaced by 'independence, well-being and personal fulfilment'[4.23]. This undermined social cohesion and replaced it with a 'pre-Victorian turbulence, backed by inequality and racial tension'. Many fortunes were being made in the retail trade, justifying Napoleon's description of the UK as a 'nation of shopkeepers', while finance and trade took over the main role from manufacturing industry, now poorly represented in league tables ranking the most wealthy. Meanwhile, a tenth of the population were living in poverty by the mid-1980s and while the middle classes were central to the UK social scene this was still not a 'middle-class country', unlike some of its continental neighbours.

Beyond the Marxist conception, the 'thing' about class that defined its culture in the UK was not a reality but more having to do with the closed minds of people in a society that was 'modern but had archaic institutions, conventions and beliefs'[4.24]. Prime Minister Major's ambition to achieve a classless society was itself evidence of a class-based nation. While the professional/managerial group in society had become the service class (or 'salariat'), the split between its two elements was deeper than in earlier times: with 'moneyed' managers being marginalised from the 'cultured' professionals[4.25].

Continual moves by the middle-class from the suburbs to the 'rural idyll' of the countryside also revealed changing cultural outlooks. Over all, the hierarchical model of class was explained by the retention 'of an elaborate formal system of rank and procedure, culminating in the monarchy itself', place in the hierarchy being defined by many other factors than just wealth. Britain's particular national mercantile culture was thus uniquely affected by aristocratic influences[4.26].

The noble heritage was kept alive by institutions such as public-schools, Oxbridge colleges and at sporting events held at Ascot, Badminton, Henley and Wimbledon, which had been kept alive by corporate sponsorship from the financial and service-industry sectors. It was argued that stately homes kept up the heritage tradition for the middle classes, visitors paying to soak up the 'immense reservoir of meaning' therein. Generally, elite groups were noted for a native hostility to rationalism and aversion to theories, which had been replaced by 'rough and ready empiricism'.

The gulf formed between management and labour in industry was, of course, not unique to the UK[4.27]. But in other societies class formalities were related to function: what stood out in the French system, for example, was that class differences were associated with greater formality and stress on dignity of title and status, a condition also recognised in the traditional US system. The more deeply entrenched indicators of class in the UK had not been challenged by strong Labour governments in the 1940s and 1960s; also in Britain a boss was often behaving as he did 'because he had been socialised into a particular social background'. No effective challenge to upper class power had existed since the passing of the Victorian industrial-owner class.

Despite a sense of 'national decline and disintegration (being) endemic' by the time of the 1977 Silver Jubilee celebrations, the event was described as 'an attempt to persuade, by pomp and circumstance, that no such decline had taken place'[4.28]. Thatcher's attempt to model an enterprise-culture on that of Victorian Britain, abandoning full employment based on a manufacturing economy, was actually 'a return of 18th century mercantilist values rather than the 19th century ones'. Thatcherism 'drew on the authority of an imagined past, with strength of contemporary desire woven in to provide a deceptive mantle of modernism'.

Heritage summoned up the splendours of the past but this helped disguise the impoverishment of the present. The common feeling of 'distrust' in management might be regarded as a mercantile tradition, whereby merchants are brought up continually to doubt the word of those with whom they deal. But trust was critically needed between individual managers in the emergent knowledge economy to capitalise on its opportunities[4.29].

Change in political culture led to a painful economic legacy

Consensus politics that had dated from the Butskellism era (*common approach to politics claimed for Rab Butler and Hugh Gaitskell*) developed into a revised form in the Heath government from 1970, but collapsed in the mid-1970s with the onset of recession. The consensus had been based on beliefs in economic growth, a mixed economy of state and private enterprises, economic planning, expanding welfare services, plus a 'corporatism' of government, the Confederation of British Industries (CBI) and Trades Union Congress (TUC). In its dying days the consensus had been weakened by a strengthening right wing faction in the Conservative Party.

The long post-war world boom had ended, with the colossal expenditure on the Vietnam War by the USA, and the massive increase in price of oil following the Yom Kippur War in the Middle East. Supplies of North Sea oil did not start to flow into the UK until 1975 so the recession conditions of the early 1970s led to a bitter battle between combinations of key trade unions and the Heath government, during which the Prime Minister sought a general election on the grounds of 'who governs Britain?'. Though inflation stood at 10% in 1978 the TUC refused to support government policies of wage restraint. Parliament had even refused sanctions against Ford Motor UK for conceding pay increases in excess of the published norm of five percent.

New Ways for Indigenous Manufacturing

By people saving less and borrowing more, consumer-demand had risen by 14% between 1981 and 1987 but by 1986 a manufacturing trade deficit of £5.5 billion had resulted, compared with a surplus sum of the same amount in 1976. Come 1989 the economy was over-heating and interest rates being hiked, and by Autumn 1990 there were signs of both another recession and of global financial markets becoming fully established. With the decline in indigenous manufacturing the government, even back in 1986, had given a grant of £125 million as an inducement to the Japanese Nissan company to set up car manufacturing in the UK.

Small to medium manufacturing enterprises (SMEs) were particularly badly affected, with the cost of capital from traditional UK equity sources higher than the industry average and even a modest capital issue could lead to loss of control of a firm[4.30]. There was also innate conservatism, excessive risk aversion with regard to manufacturing and unwillingness to evaluate prospective industrial investments in both banking and equity markets. Capital forthcoming for SMEs was often geared to the carcass value of the enterprise, in contrast to the situation with continental European Universal Banks that placed emphasis on income-earning potential.

In the UK even pledging of homes was not unusual for SME entrepreneurs. Venture capital lending in the 1980s was supposed to provide seed-corn funding of SMEs but in the event most corporate restructuring was through management buy-outs, or buy-ins, and any 'long-term nurturing' by venture capital was usually short-lived[4.31]. A major problem was that the financial sector was based on a system of highly 'liquid' markets that allowed investors quickly to recoup any investment made. Capital stock in the UK for the first half of the 1990s was only half that of Germany, which had a value-added per worker of over £30,000.

Shorter- and longer-term, economic consequences

It was *(op. cit. 4.29)* argued that repeated international borrowing by governments in order to protect currency reserves 'led to restrictions on domestic credit (for the purchase of manufactured goods), together with other demand-reducing measures affecting industry'. There were six or seven major cuts in government expenditure between 1964 and 1973, that of 1973 being £1.2 billion; all these cuts had deflationary effects. Control of money supply by hire-purchase restrictions, ceilings on bank loans and raising the bank rate all disadvantaged industry. The transfer of control of interest rates to the Bank of England in 1971 almost inevitably benefited mercantile rather than manufacturing interests. Even miscalculations by the Treasury of public borrowing requirements for 1975 and 1976 were of such huge proportions that the Labour government need not have applied for the notorious IMF loan[4.32].

By mid-1980 the Thatcherist monetary policy[4.33], which was not at first working as expected, in due course led to unemployment of three million plus the collapse of much of manufacturing industry; this was hastened by US President Nixon's earlier suspension of dollar convertibility to gold, thus effectively putting a surcharge on imports to the US. Exchange-rate freedom imposed by the UK Heath government in the early 1970s had led to huge outflows of capital[4.34], and deregulation of the financial markets by the later Thatcher government heralded the approach of a credit boom and, of course, the eventual bust that was to result in the current recession. Prior to 1986, manufacturing firms were held back not only in the established industries but also in the 'sunrise' industries[4.35], by both the lack of capital investment and lack of public spending on their products.

Government pre-occupation with controlling inflation led to a high pound in the 1980s that hampered exports, accompanied by constraints on public spending on the industrial infrastructure[4.36]. Moreover, the 1973-9 period had seen profits low and industrial militancy high, resulting in almost a decrease in productivity *(op. cit. 4.26)*. Only the 1980s adoption by industry of a more flexible production model allowed productivity to rise but even this was marred by the earlier loss of intermediate skills required of the model[4.37]. By the time of the publication of the government's Competitive White Papers in 1994 Britain was one of the poorest countries in Western Europe[4.38]. Investment per head figures showed that the UK, with the worst industrial performance figures of any OECD economy, was made worse by the reduction in tax allowances on investment. Even by 1977 sale of foreign cars on the UK market had overtaken home-produced ones[4.39].

Britain was in marked contrast in political culture to that of its rival nations, the history of the UK experience being 'political conflict without economic success'[4.40]. The method of voting allowed relatively unpopular parties to gain power; governments so elected could then effect radical changes because a majority number of parliamentary seats could be obtained with just 40% of the vote. The adversarial style of debate was symbolised in the facing benches of the government and opposition, with democratic debate consequently compromised. The New Right politics of Thatcherism included neo-liberals advocating market-force decisions and 'neo-cons' emphasising hierarchy, authority and nation.

By April 1983, Britain was for the first time a net importer of manufactured goods and by 1988 balance of trade deficits had reached a scale which in earlier times would have caused dramatic government action. But financial markets were in the ascendance following the 'Big Bang' deregulation of 1986 and, by the end of the 1980s, services as a whole took up more than two-thirds of the workforce.

Downsides of globalisation, FDI and choice of production model

Foreign direct investment (FDI) had become by the 1980s a major substitute for import/export trade, but the main trade-flows were between the 'triad' of the US, Japan and the EU and a much smaller number between newly industrialised states, so 30% of the world population accounted for 80% of FDI[4.41]. The world stock of FDI as a percentage of GDP more than doubled in the developed economies between 1980 and 1995 and most large companies at the end of the 20th century were multi-national rather than trans-national. Historically FDI, and internationalism generally, was largely prompted by early mercantile interests following the widespread adoption of free trade.

In this context, multi-national enterprises (MNEs) described firms with a strong base in one country but operating in many others, whereas trans-national corporations (TNCs) no longer had a home base but produced and marketed on a global basis[4.42]. On the downside are the instances of foreign companies driving out domestic ones, which have a higher R&D intensity or technology-transfer capability. For example, Dutch and Spanish researchers, have identified the forcing out of native entrepreneurs in Belgium as a consequence of such direct inward investment[4.43].

Where the inward investor acquires existing enterprises in a mature economy by financial take-over, the industrial sector concerned in the mature economy could be disadvantaged in the long-term[4.44]. De-industrialisation takes place with the loss of the absorbed firm, alongside that of the 'natural' shift from manufacturing to service industries. While statistics on the latter, 'natural de-industrialisation', show increasing levels of employment in the service sectors, corresponding to decreases in the manufacturing sector, part of the shift may also be explained by foreign take-over, and then subsequent closure, of indigenous firms as mentioned above.

While British MNEs also have many transplants in overseas countries, their negative side was that they reduced the value of exports from the home country and many investments had been located in protected Commonwealth countries. The UK also had too high a concentration of exports to developing countries where the demand structure does not encourage technological updating. During the 1980s outward FDI was also accompanied by a much increased outflow of purely financial portfolio investment together with a globalisation of financial dealing[4.45]. However, the UK scored second-highest in the inflow of foreign manufacturing investment; among other things the attractions being availability of relatively skilled workers and highly educated professionals. In the UK (then) 'there was little shortage of capital', and the country was a substantial net capital exporter, yet British politicians behaved as if the UK was absolutely dependent on FDI.

The relatively recent closing of Dagenham volume-car production by Ford reduced car output by almost 200,000 units/year, and GM's ending volume car production at Luton meant 150,000 units less per year, a stark reminder of the limitations of transplants to the long-term benefit of the host economy. However, the overriding financial advantages to Ford and GM transplants in 1930s Britain were those accruing to any large scale multi-national, with greater management specialization, lower R&D costs per vehicle produced, together with access to more and cheaper capital from their parent concerns.

The British system of craft/mass-production finally collapsed after 1955, following three decades of relative economic success[4.46]. However, within BLMC future export successes were confined to specialist cars: the drop in sales for mass-produced models contrasted with a stable export market for specialist cars.

Using United Nations production figures shown graphically in Fig. 7 (Appendix C) for the international motor industry, relative national performance of the leading indigenous makers during the principal transition period from Fordism to post-Fordism, the decline of most of the 'national champions' that had retained Fordism is suggested. This is in contrast to the growth seen for the Japanese Toyota company that had already adopted its version of the flexible specialisation production model. The modest growth in the French company Renault's production might be explained in part by its collaboration with Nissan later in the period, signalling an earlier enthusiasm for Japanese methods. Most of the national champion performance graphs show abnormal declines in the 1974-75 period, perhaps attributable to the oil-shocks of that time. These are accentuated in the US (GM) case perhaps due to a sharp increase in 1982 of the influx of imports and transplants to the US from foreign manufacturers. The continuous decline of the UK national champion after 1972 might suggest that forcing Fordism on to BL was ill advised.

The scale of international involvement also helped to explain the UK having the greatest number of MNEs, after the US, despite the poor performance of the home economy (*op. cit, 4.36, pp 109-112*). By 1970 eleven of the world's largest companies were UK-based, compared with eighteen for the remainder of the EEC. Among the 200 largest non-US companies worldwide, 53 were British, 43 Japanese, 25 German and 23 French. In 1971 the value of UK production overseas was over double the value of the visible export trade and all of the top 100 UK manufacturing companies had become multinational.

A UN report said that the extent of foreign direct investment (FDI) and global trading was revealed in 2001, when it was indicated that by the end of the 20th century, the ratio of foreign affiliate sales, to global GDP, would be almost 50%. The sales value was twice as high as the value of world exports of goods and services[4.47]. Thus the pattern of establishing transplants abroad to win sales in local markets overseas had begun to dwarf traditional import/export activities. In the year 2000 alone, world foreign direct investment grew by 18% over the previous year, to reach $1.3 trillion.

The main source of the inflows came from cross-border mergers and acquisitions, and those to developed countries alone amounted to over $1 trillion. The EU, USA and Japan accounted for 71% of the inflows in 2000 (and 82% of the outflows), inflows to the EU being $617 billion. Interestingly the UK overtook the US as the largest outwards investor in 1999, with France being the next largest and the US the third. Britain's passion for financial services perhaps accounts for the highest activity in foreign direct investment while the USA's principal objective is perhaps to gain access to markets, advanced production systems and high technology in overseas countries.

Distrust and individualism: malign effects of the liberal economy

The lack of a co-ordinated market economy (CME) in Britain continued to constrain industrial expansion, with co-operative mechanisms largely absent[4.48]. In Germany, by contrast, governance mechanisms had been in place 'which balanced individual interests with collective goals and allow(ed) for long-term perspectives'. An industrial culture of trust was more pronounced in Germany, with its tight regulation and strong institutional order, whereas the British form of trust was constituted on the basis of individual experiences and was a personal one rather than a system-trust, and 'Gentlemen's agreements' were felt to be no longer suited to modern socio-economic systems.

The key difference in the two countries' governance arrangements was the German reliance on private banks compared with the equity-based UK system, the former favouring long-term stability and the latter having the ultimate sanction of company take-over[4.49]. UK stakeholders had paid too much attention to financial markets in the new 'casino economy', with shares becoming 'little more than betting slips' rather than certificates of ownership. The UK had no agency for planning and co-ordinating major restructuring, with the resultant gradual death of sectors such as indigenous machine-tool and volume-car manufacturing[4.50].

Lack of teamwork and consultation in the UK was not allowing complex problems to be solved on a rational basis, but rather by 'spur of the moment' individual impulse[4.51]. The status-ridden structure of management was blamed, alongside a lack of professional training. Government response was lacking due to the diversion of effort into maintaining sterling as an internationally tradable currency, and back-bench opposition to any government initiatives in the industrial sphere. The growing 'service class', seen under Thatcherism and New Labour[4.52], was being insulated from economic forces and seeking surer ways of obtaining reward, rather than by 'inventing and making objects that people wanted to pay money for, discovering new markets that revealed new needs: complicated, time consuming and often expensive activities'.

The final decline of MG-Rover also reveals malign cultural effects

Meanwhile press-reports had argued that, after the Rover Group was acquired by BMW, the German CEO said there was a 30% gap between German and UK productivity rates during the acquisition period, despite the massive investment made by BMW in Rover plants since the acquisition. The labour market flexibility advocated by Conservatives and New Labour, which could empower employers against unions, was not the substantive issue. BMW wanted German-style flexibility with worker hours shiftable over the year as demand fluctuated, a very different concept of 'adaptability'. BMW invested £600 million/year up until 1997 compared with the £250 million/year of B.Ae. While the group was then 'breaking even' by UK accounting standards, thanks to Land-Rover's profitability, in German accounting terms this amounted to £40 million/year pre-tax loss.

By the first three months of 1995 Rover's European (including UK) car sales had slumped to 12.7% of that market and in 1995, as a whole, the UK market share had dropped to 11.4% and productivity to 14.3 cars per worker per year compared with Ford's 20.3. A BMW manager was to comment 'Rover's strengths seem to be the creation of unnecessary friction, a disappointing no-risk attitude, and an amazing display of egoism. There is obviously a culture clash between our companies'. By 1996 former CEO John Towers had left, so reinforcing Rover's immersion into BMW's culture, in a year when £600 million investment had been spent, 20% more than anticipated.

Production increased but profits decreased; BMW had been too slow at infusing their culture into Rover. By the end of 1998 BMW planned a £2 billion transfer of components purchase away from the UK but reported increased annual parts-spend of £4 million for Rover and Land-Rover, as an inevitable consequence of the high value of the pound. Early in 1995 the pound had considerably reduced in exchange value after withdrawal from the ERM but increased to D.M2.62 later. By the end of 1997 it reached D.M2.90 and mainland European Rover sales slumped. BMW's chairman urged the UK to join the EMU to reduce the value of the pound, but without success.

In March 1998 the pound hit DM3.20 and Rover was painfully exposed, the new CEO Walter Hasselkus maintaining that it could not compete with the 30% reduction in sterling competitiveness since 1996; 'the service and financial sectors of the UK economy give a false impression of what is happening in the world of real manufacturing and international competitiveness'. Rover continental sales had been three times the size of the next largest competitor so the firm was uniquely exposed. Meanwhile government was granting financial aid to Ford for its Jaguar operation but refusing it to BMW (in 1991 Ford almost closed down Jaguar following a lack of profitability after its purchase at an inflated price). Ford had cut its UK workforce from 12,800 to 7000 and then to 6000. Ford UK's satellite plant at Halewood was transferred to Jaguar manufacture so another volume-car plant had been removed, prior to Dagenham's severe down-sizing (around the time of the Alchemy negotiations to buy Rover, Ford bid almost £2bn for Land Rover, Ford itself having lost $100mn in 1999).

By that time Chancellor Brown was threatening to cut the UK's state aid offer by £50 million, while BMW insisted that at least £1.7 billion was needed to secure 11,500 Longbridge jobs. The impasse led to BMW's shock decision to sell Rover (this was soon after the sale of Land-Rover to Ford), Alchemy Partners had been named as the prospective Rover buyer, but one which was only prepared to make and sell MG specialist vehicles. BMW rightly believed that it never received the respect it deserved from the DTI as the UK's largest inward investor: there was 'latent hostility to things German at senior levels of the British establishment' yet this 'historic antipathy did not extend to the Japanese'. The DTI had an 'inadequacy in understanding the business game in which it was engaged' according to a parliamentary select committee report; they were both 'arrogant (and) unprepared because of weak intelligence'.

After Alchemy withdrew from the purchase contract, in favour of Phoenix, press reports suggested that by 2003 the financial restructuring of MG-Rover meant that the four Phoenix holding-company founders enjoyed the valuable property and financial assets of the former company, while the MG-Rover operating company bore the main burdens of the business, a situation that prompted media vilification. A year-2002 pre-tax loss of £95 million was down from the 2001 loss of £187 million but this did not prevent a trust fund being set up for the four owners, who then used it to pay themselves £3.7 million in 2001 and £15.1 million in 2002. The consequent adverse publicity helped to depress monthly sales of cars to just 2% of the UK market, in the wake of media accusations of company asset-stripping. But the drop in sales from 170,200 units in 2001 to 148,500 units in 2002 (resulting in losses for the year of £378 million) was also due to poor mainland-European sales performance, caused by the high value of the pound.

During the purchase of MG-Rover, Phoenix set up a parent company Techtronic (2000) to own the assets of the purchase, while workers received 35% and dealers 25% of the equity, the four directors sharing the other 40%. Government influence over events was negligible; in the lead up to two general elections 'it needed to be seen to help but not to compromise its non-interventionalist philosophy'. Techtronic had acquired the shares in MG-Rover, its subsidiaries and its assets for around £7.7 million in 2000, but there was a shortfall of £35.9 million between cash sent by BMW to Techtronic and the amount MG-Rover owed to Techtronic. By Autumn 2004 MG-Rover were negotiating with the prospective buyer Shanghai Automotive (SAIC).

The previous year's sales had amounted to 144,000 units but UK market share had stuck at around 2.5%. Meanwhile MG-Rover's joint venture with the Indian Tata company had been set up and city-cars made by that company were being badged as Rovers and sold in the UK. Then a rescue bid for Rover was announced by SAIC at £1.5 billion for a 70% stake in the company plus control of the assets and intellectual property. In the event SAIC became wary of the wider proposed deal and MG-Rover foolishly offered the intellectual property rights on key car models to them, effectively preventing any further buyer from future manufacture of these designs. SAIC paid just £67 million for rights to the R25 and R75 cars, probably two of the most popular models, as well as those for the company's engine and transmissions.

Some 5000 jobs were lost in the subsequent Rover collapse, though the Phoenix directors argued that they had taken over a company that nobody wanted and had sustained these jobs for five years. Nanjing Automobile became the final winner in bids for MG-Rover assets at a price of £50 million, Nanjing proposing UK assembling of MG sports cars at Longbridge, from Chinese kits, and involving a 2000-strong local workforce (that later turned out to be a few hundreds). By June 2006 Nanjing were supplying spare Rover parts and sourcing some sub-components in the UK. By February 2007 it was reported that other Rover car assembly equipment had been moved from Longbridge to Nanjing and that preparations were underway for building the MG right-hand drive sports-models in the UK.

Meanwhile it was reported that DTI inspectors at the MG-Rover government enquiry had been clocking up £12,000 per day with an estimate for the total time involved being between £5-20 million. MPMG accountants had billed the DTI £340,325 for its work and administrators PWC had earned £4 million from the Rover collapse. Auditors Deloitte had been paid £7.8 million by Phoenix between 2000 and 2003 and the government had to pay Phoenix £6.5 million for it to keep going during its final week. Monies thus paid to the financial sector and lost to government could have contributed substantially to a rescue package.

CHAPTER 5

New conditions for developing British manufacturing

The UK industrial culture inheritance

Historical research by Barnett had revealed that centuries-long traditions of disparaging industry, by the upper-middle and upper classes, had led to their steering their own progeny towards non-industrial professions. Traditionally UK industry had as a result 'promoted from within' and had an unusually high proportion of non-academically-qualified people, many of them sharing the 'aggrieved' outlook that was also often found among production workers. Few of the older generation graduates entering traditional industries had emerged unscarred from the experience of trying to work with 'practical men' in management, many of whom were generally uncooperative, and many professionally qualified people thus opted for alternative careers.

In the US factory, discipline was strict with regard to timekeeping, and workers were supervised by a different class of foremen than existed in the UK, where the foremen's role was ambiguous and uneasy. In the UK he was a weekly-paid wage earner, and not fully in senior management's confidence, yet expected to lead groups of up to fifty operatives. His authority was continuously challenged by shop-stewards and he was generally considered as having severe limitations in his abilities and personal equipment. This was in strong contrast to his US counterpart who was a key figure in the management system, on the monthly payroll and taking a prominent part in production meetings. Furthermore communication between different levels of management was superior in the US system.

Cost accounting and cost control, the basics of US management, had largely been absent from the UK system. Only with the later input of Japanese management techniques in the 1980s was the UK system able to stand up to and eventually overtake that part of the US system that had not yet been already Japanized.

UK Managing Directors then held the view that 'you can't teach management' despite the clear evidence to the contrary in the US and continental Europe. The reasoning was that in the early 19th century UK entrepreneurs had 'forged ahead without training', and, together with the effect of the public schools and ancient universities, believed that character-building was superior to imparting specialist knowledge.

Many large British companies had a bureaucracy resembling that of the Civil Service rather than a 'pushily commercial American corporation'. Middle management of the time was emphatically comfortable 'suburban middle class', characterised by 'inward looking traditionalism', and certainly not 'driven men' like their American counterparts.

In an interview with a former senior sales executive of ITT, John Flight[5.0] explained that no indigenous firms in the UK electrical industry used the Harvard Business School-type budgetary cost-control employed by Harold Geneen, CEO of ITT. Here was a foolproof system of keeping management at all levels fully aware of any products and process throughout the group that might benefit individual company operations, together with a three-four day international annual conference headed by Geneen at which company performance was fully monitored. Any product development report had to provide sales forecasts for each of the next five years, so that each relevant manager was obliged to develop a cost-accounting culture. However, this approach also had its downside and Geneen would humiliate those managers who failed to meet the costs required, in front of their colleagues, in a way that must have adversely affected any co-operative endeavour.

Recent crises increase the need for economic/cultural rebalance

If the economy is to be rebalanced in favour of the manufacturing sector, it is vital that the country's best brains and slickest operators are attracted into that sector if it is to challenge the competition of industrial nations around the world. Although a contraction in the financial sector would theoretically release more of the best brains into manufacturing, this is by no means a foregone conclusion in the light of the prevailing national and industrial cultures revealed in the previous chapters. Government inspired encouragement is thus needed.

While the cultures of the literary, educational, media and political establishments continue to look down on manufacturing careers, the need for cultural change is ever more pressing. In the 2011 MacTaggart lecture presented in Edinburgh, one of Google's top executives Eric Schmidt has offered one approach to a solution, by the abandoning the limited choice of 'luvvy or boffin' attitude to educational fulfilment apparent in the views of opinion-leaders.

Schmidt stresses the point by recalling some great entrepreneurs of the Industrial Revolution who were capable of being both engineers and poets at the same time.

The Confederation of British Industries recently called for stronger Government and City support for medium sized companies, struggling to secure credit from banks, which it was thought could boost the economy by £50bn/year within the next decade. This could emulate the German *Mitellstand,* in which firms of between £10m and £100m capital accounted for 1% of businesses but created 22% of jobs. Recent governments have focussed on start-up companies while firms employing between 50 and 500 people have largely been ignored. The CBI Director General argued that such companies need access to new kinds of finance such as that which would be available by opening the bond market to this size of firm. Such firms represent 30% of the UK's manufacturing base, he says.

Reconnecting politicians with industrial endeavour

Since the end of the British Industrial Revolution native industry has lacked the support of politicians from both left and right at both national and local level. To the trade unions, industrial owners had been the enemy. Historically, the Labour Party, political arm of the trade unions as well as the mouthpiece of the intellectual left, were hostile to industrialists on the grounds of past exploitation of human labour, the threat to both the British rural idyll and the pursuit of a social utopia. National politicians of the left were usually keen to extract the highest possible employer-contributions to National Insurance. At local government level, politicians of the far left saw industry as an institution to 'milk' for the highest possible level of taxation on industry, relative to the rates applying to residential property. This was the way to 'milk' the old enemy.

To the far right national politicians of a rural persuasion originally saw industry as the enemy of the land-owning, rent-seeking and agricultural interest, again supporting the raising of employer-contribution to National Insurance. At local level there was similarly little opposition by the right to the imposition of high industrial rates. There was also encouragement from urban land-owners to milk industry for ground rents, a course that later seemed to be followed by the science parks founded by the colleges of the ancient universities. The recent changes towards a positive approach to industry by some Conservative and most Labour leaders need nurturing by all concerned, alongside a batch of other measures to enhance the growth of existing UK manufacturing concerns.

Sustaining impetus of high-tech start-ups as well as the joy of craft

So called 'spin-off', or 'spin-out' companies from university research departments have become a valuable source for new industry start-ups in such fields as bio-technology, genetics and pharmaceutical manufacture, but since the credit-crunch banks have effectively withdrawn funds for allowing further development into medium-sized production companies. Historically banks have been very much a secondary source for industrial finance, behind flotation on the stock-market, and both strategies usually involve short-term loans or meeting the short-term demands of shareholders, for higher and quicker returns on investments. State supervised London and provincial industrial investment banks are urgently needed for the provision of longer-term capital financing. Protection is also needed against foreign investors swooping on spin-off firms and buying their research-knowledge prior to its exploitation in the UK.

New Ways for Indigenous Manufacturing

The well-documented diminishing of entrepreneurial drive and practical skills for the manufacturing sectors of the UK economy has been highlighted by design guru Jonathan Glancey who points out[5.0] that expansion of retail activity was dwarfing manufacturing growth at the beginning of the recent UK recession. He noted that a nation of consumers was overtaking the nation of producers and, furthermore, he recognised there was social deprivation as people were denied the opportunity for making things during their working lives. This was while the British relied on the Germans, Italians, French and Finns to supply heavy-duty machines, and similar goods, and while the Far East provided the 'clothes and digital gizmos we chase after'. He suggested that latent artistic talent exists in most people which could be exploited in the 'well making of what needs making'.

The need was to generate entrepreneurial activity in manufacturing and to find ways to attract the best students into engineering, and related 'making' disciplines, by discarding some of the laborious and uninspiring teaching methods that surround these subjects, and adding a substantial amount of humanities teaching for these students to improve social skills and enhance creative tendencies, by extending the duration of degree courses. Careful channelling of financial management and product development techniques into the teaching by management schools is also a must.

Within industry equality in the management hierarchy of styling and engineering directors, as well as encouraging a greater degree of cooperation between product and production engineers in the interest of making more economic designs, are also musts. Both sides of engineering should be familiar with the continental concept of 'Technik', meaning 'useful arts and manufacture' as well as the analytic tools of engineering and styling.

Economic needs for enhanced manufacturing input

Even at the end of the twentieth century, Rick Delbridge and James Lowe of the Cardiff Business School pointed out the continuing need for manufacturing industry in the UK; suggesting that a 'strong and internationally competitive economy cannot be based on services alone': the dominant economies of the US, Japan and Germany have had manufacturing at their heart, while the emergent economies of the late 20th century enjoyed rapid growth founded on their ability to produce and trade manufactured goods[5.1]. It has been recorded that the contribution of manufacturing to the UK's GDP dropped from 35% in 1960 to 21% in 1995, and its indigenous content has plummeted very considerably since 1960. Britain was the only advanced industrial nation since 1960 where growth of manufacturing output was less than growth of output of other goods and services: in this sense the scale of relative decline in manufacturing output had been a specific British phenomenon.

Kitson and Michie, of Birkbeck, University of London, argued that the case for maintaining a national manufacturing base also centred round its relatively high productivity relative to the service sector, aided by the economies of scale creating a system that is a dynamic engine of growth for the whole economy[5.2]. Production also enhanced product and process innovation and was therefore of value to those service-industry firms providing pre - and post-production services. However, while growing manufacturing economies can re-invest capital and skills, declining economies suffer weakening of skill-generation. Fostering innovation, and successful R&D of the appropriate kind, is another reason for manufacturing, since design and development cannot be furthered without a manufacturing base[5.3], say Finbarr Livesey *et al* of the Cambridge University Institute of Manufacturing who believe that developing knowledge-based high value-added businesses in design, without a production facility, could leave UK firms vulnerable to foreign competition, in that design capabilities are now already in place in the more recent manufacturing economies.

Encouraging an appropriate manufacturing culture

The requirements for industrial culture[5.4] were nicely encapsulated by the president of Sony in 1983, commenting on the UK difficulty in getting products to market: 'if the weight of invention and discovery was one, the weight to bring it to actual development was ten and the weight to produce it and bring it to world markets was one hundred. The UK situation seemed to be one in which discoverers were adulated and science considered a noble activity, and success in the marketplace came a poor second. In UK Research and Development (R&D) too much was spent on high-minded scientific 'R' and less on market-orientated 'D'.

While business management generally relied on trust, Williams *et al* suggest that since the recent credit crunch the City itself has been the victim of mistrust. The business and financial sector has latterly been considered to be the premier economic power in the UK, and even political power was becoming 'distant but also irrelevant' when viewed from the City and its neighbouring newspaper press[5.5]. Even the Chancellor of the Exchequer was obliged to appear at Guildhall during the Lord Mayor's Banquet to explain his actions over the financial year. Yet to many observers the City's core competences were seen as 'reckless gambling on the one hand and sharp practice on the other', particularly so following the credit crunch. A former broker characterised the financial sector as 'unduly devoted to profit-taking through the artificial ramping up of share price'.

21st century UK national culture hinders manufacturing revival

Will Hutton believes that deep inside the culture of British individuals is the tendency to stand in orderly queues, abide by the rules of society and rally around those unlucky enough to be out of pocket: summed up as *fair play* and the *rule of law*[5,6]. However, economic circumstances and the culture of the financial sector of the economy pushed a substantial proportion of individuals into being a part of the UK's 'private debt', since the government's moves towards the 'financial deregulation' of the 1980s. This led to more selfish attitudes among individuals. Super-high incomes in the financial sector are causing one of the highest rich to poor income ratios in the world, which is found to cause great stress to low-income families among the ten million adults earning less than £15,000/year. This was evidenced by Wilkinson and Pickett's book, *The Spirit Level: Why Equality is better for Everyone*, published by Penguin in 2010.

Press hysteria ensures there is little opposition to 'two nation' Britain, with social engagement being 'reduced to penal and oppressive interventions' such as CCTV policing of both the fortresses of the rich and the desolate housing estates of the poor. Some fifty percent of top journalists are privately educated but send their less-prosperous minions, along with the paparazzi, to terrorize their victims, in all social classes, if they can find 'evidence' against them. The most alarming problem for Britain, Hutton maintains, lies in the 'herd-like, populist, conservative media that disregards the impartiality of fact, does not hold the powerful to account, trivialises the quest for objectivity . . . and trashes plurality'.

At the heart of the present predicament in relation to UK entrepreneurial culture, two elites are cited as having influenced British industrial development since World War II: trade unions until the early 1980s and the City of London thereafter. The former used their privileged position in the British state to seize as much economic advantage as they could, during successive governments' fear of unemployment. However, when Prime Minister 'Thatcher successfully attacked the unions' privileged position . . . (she) then allowed the financiers to take their place - although the latter's colonisation of the state was more subtle'

Stimulating a change in the national culture

Gradually the cultural attitudes towards 'class' and 'caste' are changing in the UK. However, official census statistics group people in classes defined by income and occupation, while advertising classifications will divide people according to their lifestyles and buying tastes. Commentators frequently confuse these quite separate interpretations of 'class'. Perceptions of class and caste have perhaps been revealed by the former French observer de Tocqueville who had seen the British, over the centuries, as needing to 'have someone beneath them' as vehemently as a Frenchman dreads 'having anyone above him'. Politicians of all parties are hopefully fully cognisant of caste effects as well as class effects.

A significant cause of Britain's economic decline has been attributed to the loss to industry, possibly affected by relocation from town to country, of the second and subsequent generations of successful industrialists. The towns and cities, with their associated industries, are very much the losers, as not only are industrial entrepreneurs disappearing, but also valuable middle-management and specialist-professionals desert the urban environment and become deeply entrenched in the rural 'heritage culture'. During the Industrial Revolution period artisans, and industry middle-managers/specialists largely shared an urban culture that fostered manufacturing. Now these two groups seemed to have divided in *perceived* class and caste terms.

This intertwining of cultural-class with economic-class is an important concept in understanding modern UK class-consciousness. If there is disharmony between classes, and perhaps even occasional class 'warfare', it is clearly the perception of class that matters to the protagonists, not the socio-economic definitions. A more formal ordering of society in terms of occupation would be a preferable alternative to the British norm of recognising caste and taste more than formal economic class divides. Minimising the middle-class rural/urban divide by refurbishing the urban environment, nurturing citizen service to the urban community, and encouraging members of the backward-looking 'service class' back into the mainstream urban culture would seem to be generally beneficial.

Questioning the certainties of UK industrial culture

The proffered solution of imposing an American-style business culture on British industry and consumer outlets is not always the answer. The American culture is one of 'move-in, make your mark, and move off', which US directors ingrain into their managerial staff. It is a harsh business climate which possibly comes from a predominately immigrant people who have endured hardship in their original homelands, subsequently finding themselves somewhat dispossessed and having to make their mark, 'hard and fast', in their New World.

Similarly, American-cultured managers show very little sympathy for accommodating to the native culture, when posted overseas. Perhaps the same could also be said of early British Empire colonizers as is now being said of the industrial colonizers of the global economy.

There is a superficial layer of apparent 'equality' between managers and managed in American-style culture but beneath it is a hard impersonal brashness that spells insincerity in the general approach and which certainly does not draw the best from British workers. British industry perhaps needs to adopt a continental corporate culture rather than a trans-Atlantic one.

Historically the British class system has regarded the professional middle classes as being superior to the perceived 'level' of industry managers and specialists. The talent and dedication of members of the traditional professional middle class is thus increasingly lost to an industry desperately needing to compete effectively with its mainland-European, American and Asian rivals. The relentless application of our competitors to marketing and quality-control has to be somehow matched, and overtaken, by British industrial managements.

The latter are, by default, losing the professional skills of their forebears as their modern equivalents escape into more socially-prestigious occupations. There is a dangerous mythology afoot that a large number of the working population can step into high added value high-technology jobs, even while our education system has been neglected for so long that great sections of society are barely literate or numerate. The need above all is to attract the highly educated élite, back into industry from their prestige jobs in the media, the 'City' and the entertainment world: perhaps regaining the respect which has deserted UK industrialists since the Industrial Revolution.

A slimmer monarchy to diffuse 'establishment' power

Anyone in doubt about the effect of the UK national culture on the manufacturing spirit of the nation had only to witness the

New Ways for Indigenous Manufacturing

BBC-television report on the Jubilee pageant taking place on the River Thames. Here, for anyone concerned with how the national backdrop against which the unemployed youth desperately search for work in industry, was the British Establishment in all its glory. On display was evidence of how the real holders of power in Britain squander vast sums of money, which might be used to restructure industry so it could flourish in the new circumstances for the world economy, being spent on a spectacle seemingly designed to raise the spirits of a public by being exposed to the glorification of aristocratic tradition.

The much loved British queen, who has carried the burden of office for sixty years, might have enabled the admiration and respect of every one of her subjects had she been involved in a simpler ceremony for herself and her husband without the expensive pomp involved in the glorification of her wider family. This is a family supported by a burgeoning aristocracy and a huge cadre of upper-crust public servants seemingly devoted to maintaining a culture that serves past history much more intently than any present day one. It must be a considerable cause of embarrassment to the few politicians and officials who are finally coming to terms with the massive task of redirecting the national culture towards resuscitating UK manufacturing. That was the part of the country's economy that could reverse the trend towards mass unemployment, rather than hiding behind a glorious past. Much of the general public needs growth rather than grandeur.

Despite the UK public's seeming detraction from almost everything in mainland Europe, under pressure from the right-wing media, what is left of the continental monarchy seems to operate in an admirable way, without ignoring the needs of industry in the individual countries concerned. The Swedish royal family, with its involvement in the Nobel Prize, has a world influence on economic progress as well as being the figurehead of a country noted for its industrial prowess.

Without going to the unpopular length of a move to full republicanism, it seems entirely possible that politicians might eventually see their way to removing medieval titles from the Honours List, adopting a Scandinavian-style monarchy which does not require or desire a supporting aristocracy, slimming down the expensive pageantry and processions that broadcast caste-divides, and branding the working majority as citizens rather than subjects.

Tackling the sacred cow of land ownership

The structure of land-ownership might also be reformed without resorting to full nationalisation of land, by allowing long-term tenant farmers, for example, to purchase farm land from the large estates on favourable terms through a conditional subsidy. Large landowners could offset income from the government for the care of amenity land as a measure of compensation for farm rents lost. In urban areas there may eventually be legislation to allow councils to acquire land freeholds in the long term, so that residents and industrialists would eventually just buy the leaseholds of their properties, with democratically controlled ground rents. This would have the valuable effect of reducing land speculation, and the unjustified profits made by speculators when land is re-zoned by councils from one use to another, while protecting industry from extortionate rents.

Landed titles could disappear with sensible reform of the House of Lords into a senate similar to that in the US, and eventually dropping the Honours List in its heraldic form, with mandatory ending of inherited titles and disestablishment of the Church thereafter. This would require the Church being given the opportunity for its authorities to sell off redundant buildings and obtain government assistance in maintaining properties of historic and aesthetic importance. Posts such as Lord-Lieutenant of a county could very usefully fall to the leader of the county council, or his/her appointee. And the many medieval 'heraldic-type' posts could safely disappear in favour of more contemporary equivalents, to remove the 'living in the past' aura which overseas visitors recognise in Britain.

Respect for patriotic endeavour in the form of service to the community would eventually replace sycophantic worship of descendents of the squirarchy and nobility. False egotism, pride and chauvinism seen in British culture by foreigners would then perhaps be seen to be gradually eliminated. Land reforms would eventually displace a rentier culture that has sustained the ruling class and undermined its middle class aspirants of productive occupations, hopefully causing a trickle-down effect through the middle classes that would make a considerable slice of them less inclined to ape the aristocratic culture.

In a newspaper report Will Hutton has championed this form of land reform, but in the shape of a 'right to buy' policy paralleling the earlier legislation applying to council-house tenants. It argues that the New Right landlord-friendly rent 'reforms' of the mid-1990s, coupled with widespread avoidance of inheritance tax, has further monopolised land ownership by the rich and powerful. Perhaps some form of land reform could also be extended to urban estates, industrial and retail as well as residential. Substantial handouts offered to overseas inward investors should also be accompanied by a careful nurturing of native industries in the crucial formative stage. Urgent attention is also needed to prevent research-based firms having to sell their skills abroad at too early a stage in product and company development.

Reforming government policies and institutions

UK government should stage a withdrawal from Britain's historic world role, and water down the 'special relationship' between the UK and the US, to achieve a reduction in armament expenditure and the redirecting of military R&D towards improving industrial competitiveness. A rethink of international policy should give emphasis to trading between countries and providing control over the financial sector to reduce the prevalence of foreign transplants in the UK and to recognise, for example, that FDI deprives indigenous industry of the financial benefit of exports. Above all government should drive its economic management towards the goal of maximising economic stability for industry.

An unquestioning attitude towards the 'free market' should also be addressed as should the continual cultural emphases on hierarchy, authority and militaristic nationalism. The unfortunate effect of the 'Big bang' deregulation of 1986 on present-day industrial performance has escaped the attention of opinion-leaders, until very recently, with dire consequences. Above all there is a need to move towards a co-ordinated market economy, instead of a liberal market economy, with 'system-trust' taking over from the unreliable 'gentleman's agreement' trust once prominent in the UK.

There is insufficient recognition that reforms such as those urged by the Chartists as long ago as the early 19th century have still not been fully introduced by any UK government. The reforming organisation Charter 88 has thus recommended among its proposals: to create a fair electoral system of proportional representation, to reform the upper house to establish a democratic, non-hereditary second chamber, to place the executive under the power of a democratically renewed parliament and all agencies of the state under the rule of law, also to draw up a written constitution, anchored in the idea of universal citizenship, which incorporates these reforms.

Reforming industrial democracy

Fostering unity across the industrial-manager/worker 'class-divide' by encouraging worker shareholding and participation in industrial decisions have been key lessons in management studies. There was also a parallel need for redirecting, by in-service training, the remaining 'practical men' in their new role of a modern manager. Widespread institution of weekly conferences, of workers and departmental managers, alongside workers daily discussion with team leaders, are also considered valuable by the increased adoption of the flexible specialisation production model. Furthermore, having politician, fund-manager and banker representatives on boards of directors should provide some control over hostile industrial acquisitions, as would strengthened powers for the Monopolies and Mergers Commission.

Wage bargaining should be encouraged at plant - rather than national-level and a new culture instituted that allows managers to be respected for their professionalism rather than their perceived rank in society, while workers are assisted in being better task-motivated and more flexible in developing new skills. Retaining founder-owners of expanding companies as board chairmen, in the German manner, would allow executive-directors to benefit from their advice without losing executive control. Benefit would also come from distinguishing the engineer from the technician in the professional hierarchy and ensuring works foremen promoted from the shop-floor are fully familiar with best management practice defined in the flexible specialisation production model. It is also necessary to eradicate hostile management attitudes towards the employment of well educated people holding equivalent or subordinate positions, a form of inverted snobbery that drives well-qualified people away from industry.

A seminal plea from the workshop

A 1970s study by Alan Chatterton and Ray Leonard[5.7], two professional engineers who worked in manufacturing, provides a glimpse to the uninitiated of how class-ridden, as well as culturally divided, was the industrial environment, which will be seen by many as still recognisable. Both authors started their careers as shop-floor apprentices, before reaching professional status, and they say in their introduction that they 'unequivocally hold in high regard the skills, comradeship and inherent ability of the British worker . . . and when their skills are effectively used for the common good of the whole firm, the British worker' could be unrivalled.

Work study pioneer FW Taylor is castigated for only meeting the *materialistic* needs of the capitalist economy, and his tendency to equate men and women with machines. Above all, it is argued, he failed to consider the questions of the structure of industry, and how it corresponds with man as a human-being, about the nature of man as a social animal and the basic needs of man as an individual. The so-called 'born leaders' (*traditional managers*) exploited their positions in undesirable ways and a pattern was established of leaders avenging themselves on those below them for all the indignities they had suffered from their superiors in earlier times.

Traditional British organisations were built on a structure of authority, with the worker naturally disliking many of the controls under which he/she worked. Lack of freedom is the debilitating factor. In Japan and the USA the cultural value of equality is treasured, in respect of equal rights and privileges with respect to neighbours. This value does, however, recognise individual mental, emotional and social differences; hence differing rewards are granted and employers tend to oppose favouritism and personal privilege. Britain's crucial fault is to accentuate class differences, a situation easily recognised by foreigners but to which most Britons remain blinded.

> The authors state: *traditional UK management philosophy had been built on the notion that workpeople are like children, with work situations being defined by dependence and constraint. Steep pyramidal structures were the norm with all orders and instructions coming from the top downwards and 'management knows best'. Departmental managers thus benefited by keeping as much information as possible to themselves. Junior managers tended to be uninformed and shop-floor leadership was negative, arising from their own sense of insecurity. General distrust leads to communication failure and distortion of translated information in both downward and upward directions. A subordinate's future is seen by him to depend on how well he knows his boss and the information passed upwards is tempered to reflect as well as possible on the subordinate. In the end the chief executive can be quite misinformed on essential company matters and line managers tend to rely on exhortation and show very little self-involvement with the task they are setting. Shop-floor workers produce because they are required to do so, and usually 'at half steam', instead of being motivated to do so.*

Chatterton and Leonard say that while the 1870 Education Act was set up partly to resist the growing competitive threat from the Germans and Americans, it was pursued under an ethos of strict systematic discipline leading to producing the obedient worker. Upper and middle classes were subjected to longer uninterrupted periods of education which, it is believed, resulted in the members of these classes having greater bellicosity than members of the working class. The 1944 Education act was intended to bring about a parity of esteem but had failed to do so, they considered. A variant on modern comprehensive schools was proposed: that the grammar schools be reinstated but the top 20% of all junior schools should attend them, both those in good areas and those in bad areas, arguing that this would lead to a university population which resembled the social mix of the population as a whole (*though some cognisance should be made of highly successful primary schools in ancient-university-cities, or other progressive cities, where up to 80% of worthwhile pupils could be lost to the system*).

Reform of the British education system

Debates about UK educational change tend to be carried on within separate streams, at each side of a cultural divide between arts and science. Such a divide also separates the 'pure' from the 'applied', natural from the physical sciences, and the humanities from the social sciences. The separation between the arts intelligentsia, and the technological specialists, who have each developed their separate cultures, can mean their own languages are scarcely intelligible to one another. These debates are often conducted without any reference to international benchmarks and can ignore the fact that other nationalities often enjoy better integration between what some Britons regard as 'opposing' cultures.

However, recent media debates have favoured an integrated approach to arts - and science-education in the UK, seen as contributing towards a greater international competitiveness for British industry. Overcoming communication blocks between industry personnel can be helped in the four or five year undergraduate courses proposed for some of the technological disciplines. Students of applied science should have built into their courses a much greater understanding of the social sciences, and literature, to prepare them for the realities of industrial life. The other aim of such courses was intended to give technologies professional equality with such disciplines as law and medicine, providing studies leading to qualifications for management-grade, alongside specialist-grade, applied scientists.

School-level educational reforms need priority

According to newspaper reports former Prime Minister Blair had talks with the High Master of Manchester Grammar School, Dr Stephen, with a view to discussing possibilities for opening up independent school sixth forms to students from the state sector. Dr Stephen favoured bringing 120 former direct-grant schools back into the state sector as specialist academic centres of excellence, which perhaps prompted the Labour party to set up the academies programme. It was also suggested that the usual pattern of the best Comprehensive Schools being in the 'best' suburban middle class areas is sometimes broken by the existence of exceptionally high performing inner-city Comprehensives. By examining performance statistics it was confirmed that the best Comprehensives are those *having the best feeder primary schools* at the top of the league tables, and not just dependent on the prosperity of the area. To improve widespread literacy and numeracy an overriding national objective must therefore be to raise primary school standards 'across the board'.

A theme of Japan's attitude to education has been that, with the country being short of natural resources, it had to make up for this by the power of education, according to a newspaper report. In 1982 nine percent of the country's income went on education compared with 1% on defence. In contrast with the UK philosophy of eschewing change in favour of preserving proven methods, Japan, whose children outscore most others on international tests of intelligence, send 5000 teachers abroad each year to learn new methods, particularly in respect of fostering creativity. Around 95% of children stay on at school and of those aged 15 years and over 35% go on to higher education. All children follow a broad, general course and there is no selection until fifteen.

There is no vocational-content, this being generously provided by Japanese commerce and industry, but science is part of the elementary school curriculum. Even after 15 years of age, two-thirds of those staying on take broad academic courses leading to university. Courses at university then take four years and again general studies are pursued during the first two years. The school curriculum includes group ethics, co-operation, loyalty, responsibility to others, and pupils learn public responsibility by being made, with their teachers, to clean school rooms and grounds.

Another press-report has a solicitor specialising in charity law observing that the Downing Street Strategy Unit has been somewhat complacent in its turn-of-the - century review of the charity and voluntary sectors, particularly with respect to the responsibilities of independent schools towards the community at large. However, this review left the door open for reform, by instancing the application of the public benefit test in terms of pupil exchanges and joint activities with the maintained sector, in order to 'dismantle a little of our educational apartheid'. There was also the quoted requirement that 'independent schools which charge high fees have to make significant provision for those who cannot pay full fees' in order that these schools should be allowed to retain their charitable status.

University level reforms focus on technology

Department of Trade and Industry (DTI) studies indicated that Britain's poor productivity record compared to Germany and the US was due to a shortage of skills among manufacturing workers in the high-technology industries. The introduction of foundation degrees in the UK helped to accredit technologists and others who had advanced from technician grade and gave them the opportunity to qualify within a two year course. It was generally accepted that a foundation degree graduate could obtain an honours degree within a further four terms of study.

Recent attempts to introduce industrial technology into the national curriculum had met with little success, technology becoming diffused, as more linkages with arts, crafts, business studies, IT and home economics were required[5.10]. The only initiatives for technical education in recent years have been a plethora of failed youth employment schemes, many of which undermined the remaining apprenticeship schemes. High dropout rates also suggested a low calibre of candidates and it has led to the decline of other qualifications such as the BTEC National Diplomas. In general vocational education and training (VET) has been difficult to implement because of the poor differentials between skilled and unskilled labour and the reluctance of private-sector companies to support the schemes on offer, leading to Britain being trapped in a 'low skills equilibrium'.

Of the 'newer' universities, Warwick has been the most successful in forging industrial links, particularly in engineering and management relating to the automotive and electrical industries. The remainder were established in the outskirts of cathedral cities and have concentrated on the liberal arts and social sciences. The newer technical universities that grew out of the CATs had tended to drop technology from their titles following the sharp swing away from technology as the choice of study for their applicants. This is attributed to the lack of A-levels being awarded in science and mathematics with the slow wastage of teachers in those subjects. This in turn has historical explanation in the decline in real wages of teachers, *vis-à-vis* manual workers, in the early post-war Labour government. In 1985 not one Cambridge physics graduate chose teaching as a career. A vicious circle of decline arose, the result of which was that the preferences of sixth formers were allowed to determine government policy whether it was in the national interest or not. Even the polytechnics veered away from technology, a 1970s survey showing polytechnics having a higher level of arts publications than the universities.

Recent press reports say one of the problems for UK society arises from the undergraduate education system at 'Oxbridge', which had been described as 'finishing schools for the gilded youth of Britain's upper middle classes'. Despite moves by the government to query the public funding of collegiate education, a massive lobbying campaign had again put off the day when students were surcharged for this special privilege. This source even suggests there is a case for turning Oxbridge into post-graduate institutions. Back in the 1970s there was a related broadcast discussion as to whether or not 'public school' values had any place in industry. While some would argue that the sound of the accent would accentuate class hostility in an industrial dispute situation, others felt that the confidant style of leadership such schools were said to imbue would be a useful recompense, in that the person relates better to workers because he is more at ease.

A TUC official added to the debate that '. . . the new school tie is worse than the old school tie . . .', the former he saw as 'saloon-bar Toryish types telling stories about work-shy people' . . . (such types being a) . . . 'bigger impediment to British industrial efficiency'. He suggested that the tension between their backgrounds and their new managerial status make them highly critical of workers whereas the old-school-tie types could be more open-minded. The new-school-tie debater retorted that '. . . they mean it is easier to take advantage of an amateur with a guilt complex . . .'. A merchant banker in the debate even suggested that there is a 'terrible reverse censorship against old Etonians', for example, despite the first class academic record at Eton, and school leavers could almost finish up with an inferiority complex. An executive-head-hunter in the debate suggested that 'some sections of industry tended to carry mediocrity because it was socially acceptable and to be uncomfortable with better performers because they were too challenging'.

Requirements for the knowledge economy

According to the prominent industrial organisation guru, Peter Drucker of the Claremont Graduate University Management School, the educated person in the unfolding Knowledge Economy need(ed) to 'understand the (various) knowledges (subjects)'; this is not so much as a polymath but to be able to have a grasp of what each is about[5.9]: 'its central concerns/theories, its major new insights, important areas of ignorance, its problems and challenges'. The knowledge economy had in part come about from the post World War 2 action, in the USA, of the GI Bill of Rights that granted ex-servicemen fees to attend university. This move has been responsible for giving the US the lead in the emerging new technologies, which were to transform the economy and society by the end of the 20th century. The Knowledge Economy makes the 'organisation in general', and the industrial firm in particular, worthy of study and a multi-disciplined approach to its study would have been a useful exercise.

The requirement for divided responsibility among team-members in such an organisation means that each individual needs to take responsibility for objectives, contribution and behaviour of the organisation as a whole, demanding a good command of subjects beyond his or her own particular discipline. Such an economy marks the change from knowledge being always concerned about 'being' to a new phase in which it is about 'doing'. In Britain patents were first granted to encourage the application of knowledge to products and processes, which began to reveal to a wider public the hidden wonders of 'craft'. Key elements of knowledge (both tacit and non-tacit) need to be imparted to youngsters in schools, also throughout adult life. The school needs to provide universal literacy and numeracy of a high order, a command of several languages, and to imbue students of all ages with motivation to learn. A university has not just to be open to people who have recently left school or college but also to those who did not gain access to higher education in their earlier years.

A valuable DTI report in 1999[5.10] claimed that *'information only becomes knowledge when it has been assimilated and understood. How the information is interpreted and used will vary according to the experience, expertise and skills of the people accessing it. An important distinction is often made between 'codified' and 'tacit' knowledge. Knowledge is codifiable if it can be written down and transferred while tacit knowledge is often slow to acquire and much more difficult to transfer, for example familiarity with a particular production process or management practice or knowledge of customer needs and preferences. By its nature, tacit knowledge or 'know-how' can be an important source of competitive advantage. Increasing dependence on the generation and exploitation of both types of knowledge for wealth creation is the characteristic of today's knowledge-driven economy.*

148

The growing importance of knowledge as a determinant of manufacturing performance is being driven by four mutually reinforcing factors that are changing the nature of competition and the way manufacturers do business: revolutionary changes in ICT (information and communication technologies); more rapid scientific and technological advance; global competition and changes in tastes and lifestyles that arise from increased incomes. Consumers now demand more sophisticated, and often more customized products, all of which require greater flexibility and greater use of knowledge. Sustainability is also driving pressures for change in existing ways of doing business. Rising environmental and social expectations are coming from both governments and the marketplace, and are likely to intensify as the world grows both richer and more populous'.

Reform of the financial sector

In an urban society, encouraging co-operation between politicians, financiers, entrepreneurs and work-people at regional-government level rather than county level, would be more effective in fostering industrial development. Urging the French model of 'indicative planning' on to local and national government politicians and managers would also help. (*Wikipedia describes indicative planning as a form of central economic planning implemented by a state in an effort to solve the problem of imperfect information in economies and thus increase economic performance*). When utilizing indicative planning, the state employs influence, subsidies, grants, and taxes (to affect the economy), but does not compel. It is quite different from *directive* or *mandatory planning*, where a state sets quotas and mandatory output requirements. The 'indicative' method of economic planning originated in France after the Second World War.

New Ways for Indigenous Manufacturing

At national level, investment-fund managers should at least make an input to policy-making in industrial firms through non-executive directorships. There is a need to prevent hostile take-overs of companies and, following the methods used by continental industrialists to discourage unproductive mergers, to concentrate instead on improving productivity rather than asset acquisition through merger. Changing the culture of financial institutions through a measure of state-control over the cost of investment capital, and a reduction in the cost of foreign exchange to industry, would represent significant improvements, as would regulating the use of leveraged buy-outs involving just the exchange of ordinary shares.

Meanwhile the urgent need for industrial investment banks under government supervision should also be recognised, particularly in aiding SMEs that often have to suffer the pledging of their founder's homes to secure finance. City livery companies should be encouraged to promote better understanding between financial, trade and manufacturing interests rather than just being involved in *mercantile* specialisms. Closer alignment between government, civil service, industry and its sales outlets is also urgently needed, particularly when severe financial difficulties face particular enterprises.

Hutton has argued that the 'destructive relationship between British finance and industry' had been identified as the long-term factor most affecting manufacturing decline, a situation that was not matched in the US states, despite the divide at federal level between finance and industry[5.11]. At local and regional level US banks *did* invest in industry. There was also nothing in the UK to compare with the 'developmental' state of Japan, and UK industry was condemned to maximise short-term returns to satisfy the financial markets. At state and city level in the US there was still a kind of moralism in medium-sized corporations, like in Germany, that was quite absent in the UK, where the new generation of business leaders held the view that they owed the workforce none of the profits. When they saw the profits dipping UK directors even sold their own shares in the concern before others had proper knowledge of international financial markets[5.12].

The recent credit crunch and parliamentary expenses crisis have actually precipitated moves towards constitutional reform for both the institutions of government and the financial sector. An *Observer* leading article asserted that: *'to get "good" British long-term owners of industrial assets requires creating structures of corporate law, shareholder responsibilities and long-term lending that the City has always opposed. Such structures threaten margins in the financial services industry and the City's international position, which is still considered more important than the UK industrial base and, by inference, the wages and living standards of UK workers'.*

Need for UK to change from being a Liberal Market Economy

According to Cristel Lane there are now being voiced both triumphant claims and fears that one model of capitalism - that of competitive or liberal market economy (LME) - is displacing all other models[5.13]. Of the two major approaches to corporate governance, the first approach, current in mainstream economics, is only concerned with the relationship between financiers of firms - mainly shareholders and banks (principals) - and their agents (managers) while the second, more common outside economics, is the stakeholder approach. This focuses on the entire network of formal and informal relations which determines how control is exercised within corporations.

The former is equated with outsider and arms' length control, connected with dispersed share ownership and the prevalence of institutional investors. The latter, dwelling on the whole network of control, occurs when share ownership is more concentrated and owners of significant portions of ownership are able to exercise insider control. Concentrated holdings may be held by family owners, banks or other non-financial firms. In the insider system, control is exercised through board membership and legal rights of appointment and dismissal. For corporate control, and in the threat of take-over, such a system is said to be more direct and active, whereas in the outsider system control is indirect and exerted via the market. Regrettably the outsider system also allows for the goals of liquidity of capital markets and of opportunities for short-term maximisation of returns on capital invested.

The essence of the traditional insider system in Germany has been described by Cristel Lane as follows: *among sources of capital for German firms retained earnings have been the most significant, leaving firms highly autonomous. Bank debt was low, and issuing of shares through listing on the stock market was common only among a small proportion of the largest firms. During the period of 1982 to 1991, (starting before the 'big-bang' UK financial deregulation in 1986) German stock market capitalisation stood at only 20 per cent of GDP, compared with 75 per cent in the UK. Ownership in German firms has been relatively concentrated, and family ownership was still significant even in some very large firms. Cross ownership of non-financial firms has been more pronounced and interlocking directorships have been highly developed. For all these reasons, hostile take-over was almost unknown.*

. . . . a good pattern for an industry-friendly economy.

APPENDIX A

Towards an enhanced motor-industry specialist sector

With the demise of MG-Rover in 2005 there seemed to be little prospect of expansion for smaller scale indigenous motor vehicle manufacturing industry. Yet despite the steady decline of the indigenous volume sector since the 1980s, there had traditionally been a relatively strong *specialist* motor vehicle sector, since the 19th century beginnings of UK motor manufacture. It blossomed into a substantial indigenous racing car design-and-build sector during and beyond the 1990s. This also has an accompanying high-performance road-car element that could be beneficially expanded and further developed for lower cost solutions with electric vehicles (EVs).

Electric car development, for wider acceptance by the market, depends upon achieving acceptable range at reasonable cost. Skilled technologists and technicians working in medium sized firms may become inheritors of this task, rather than the 'boffins' of the start-up firms or the specialist researchers of the large corporations, although the later two categories have of course produced high-performance *concept* EVs not yet in production. For medium-sized companies it would be essentially a development task in turning scientific research into high-efficiency final products. This should have appeal to British ingenuity among former skilled automotive-, and similar engineering-workers, seeking employment and frustrated by the limited job-satisfaction, and indeed the very existence of work, in some declining indigenous volume-production industries.

The UK Society of Motor Manufacturers (SMMT) does not discuss pure electric vehicles on its web-site but has usefully described the hybrid EV as representing three categories of vehicle: Plug-In Hybrid Vehicles (PHVs) having battery range in excess of 10 miles, after which they revert to *hybrid* capability, using battery and Internal Combustion Engine (ICE) power for propulsion; Extended-Range Electric Vehicles (E-REVs) are similar, but they have a shorter battery range of around 40 miles which is extended by an ICE on-board generator, providing additional mileage capability. Unlike PHVs, which can use electric or full hybrid for propulsion, E-REVs always use electricity for propulsion and probably an IC engine for on-board battery charging. SMMT say eligible vehicles sold in the UK for the Plug-In Car Grant are Mitsubishi i-MiEV, Smart four-two electric drive, Peugeot iOn, Nissan LEAF, Citroën C-Zero, Tata Vista, Vauxhall Ampera, Toyota Prius Plug-In and Chevrolet Volt.

Revised approaches to the specialist electric-car business had been suggested over a decade ago by Scott Cronk, Business Development Director at US Electricar (*Building the E-motive Industry: Essays and Conversations about Strategies for Creating an Electric Vehicle Industry*, Society of Automotive Engineers, 1995). He argued that lower volume production rates involved a quite different set of component and system suppliers than would be required for servicing a specialist manufacture of this nature. The need for a battery/fuel-cell charging infrastructure different from petrol stations also serves to distinguish electric vehicles as a separate culture. Purchase price will be higher and resale price probably lower due to obsolescence in the face of advancing technology, he suggested. The notion of periodically billing the customer for an on-going personal mobility could be preferable to just selling him/her a car in the normal way.

New Ways for Indigenous Manufacturing

The customer would be thus spared the business of bargaining with dealers, obtaining finance, insurance and registration as well as the bother of refuelling and making arrangements for periodic servicing. Periodic servicing would be extended to 50,000 mile intervals for specialist electric vehicles, and systems for refurbishing high mileage vehicles with updated technology systems might well be possible. The interlinking of mobility providers by horizontal networks would obviously benefit the customer as he/she travels from one area to another, possibly using different transport modes. The provider might be a sort of cross between travel agent and customer liaison officer of a motoring organization, but principally the leaser of the vehicle, Cronk forecast.

In manufacturing the electric vehicle a different perception of original equipment manufacturer, from that of the conventional car assembler, would be apparent, because it was likely to be a company much smaller in size than that of its key specialist system suppliers, who will probably serve many other industries as well. The original equipment manufacturer could possibly become systems integrator for a partnership chain of long term suppliers and appoint a project leader to coordinate design, development and production, leading a cross-company team. Such leadership would carry the authority for detailed cost investigations in any of the member firms.

Electric vehicle leasers would need to network with manufacturing project leaders and provide carefully researched hire schedules of potential lessees upon which series production could be planned. This would be without need for large parks of finished vehicles, which conventional OEMs use as a buffer between supply and demand, as well as their need to maintain excess idle production capacity in slack periods. Organizational innovation thus shares similar importance with technological innovation, in electric vehicle production.

New Ways for Indigenous Manufacturing

By the start of the 21st century, fuel-cell and battery-powered vehicles had mostly still been the province of off-shoot departments of volume producers, but the market was only in the early stage of development. In the UK, where electrical manufacture has been looked upon favourably as a 'laboratory-based' industry, rather than having the traditional 'blacksmith' image of the motor industry, there may be future scope for electric vehicle projects coming out of existing electric traction firms or even high-tech start-up firms able to develop sophisticated control technologies.

The principal outlet, for high-performance specialist EVs, is to the customer attracted by the prospect of a virtually noiseless vehicle interior as well as the satisfaction of his/her vehicle being pollution free, as Britain catches up with its continental and trans-Atlantic neighbours in the construction of pv solar-cell farms and the proper filtration/disposal of power-station emissions.

In an earlier work the author suggested that one of the key factors for effective EVs was the need for a combination of electromotive technology along with the kind of structural expertise that went into the USA Supercar programme of the 1990s (*more recently the highly successful ventures of Gordon Murray Design discussed below*). The former was aimed at enabling unusually low fuel consumption by means of very low-drag cars and extreme lightweight construction (Hodkinson/Fenton, *Lightweight electric/hybrid vehicle decline*, Pt 2, Butterworth Heinemann, 2001). For the automotive engineer with background experience of an IC-engine prime-moving power source, the electrical aspects associated with engine ignition, starting and powering auxiliary lighting. Such work also included occupant comfort/convenience devices and all have often been the province of resident specialists within the automotive design office, which will presumably eventually fall to main-line electrical engineers involved in core propulsion systems.

In terms of reducing vehicle weight, to gain greatest benefit in terms of range from electromotive power, there also needs to be some rethinking of traditional design approaches by automotive engineers. Aerospace designers perhaps have a different instinctive approach and think of light weight and structural integrity as priorities. The discipline of early aeronautical design engineers whose prototypes either flew or fell out of the sky led them to pioneer techniques of thin-walled structural analysis to try to predict as far as possible the structural performance of parts *before* they left the drawing board (now the CAD/CAM system), and in so-doing usually economized on any surplus mass. These structural analysis techniques gave early warning of buckling collapse and provided a means of idealization, which allowed load paths to be traced.

Finite-element analysis is of course sufficiently well advanced to prove the effects of changing body structure shapes well ahead of prototype-build. However, traditional aeronautical design calculations are useful for giving design engineers a 'feel' for the structures at the concept stage and thus make crucial styling and packaging decisions without the risk of weakening the structure or causing undue weight gain. While familiar to civil and aeronautical engineering graduates, these theory-of-structures techniques are often absent from courses in mechanical and electrical engineering, which may be confined to the study of the mechanics-of-solids in their teaching.

Marketing the electric vehicle (EV)

In this period of important decision making throughout the infant EV industry, it is thus valuable to focus on the very broad range of other factors, economic, ergonomic, aesthetic and even political, which have to be examined alongside the engineering-science factors. Since the electric vehicle has thus far, in marketing terms, been 'driven' by the state rather than the motoring public it behoves the stylist and product planner to shift the emphasis towards the consumer and show the potential owner the appeal of the vehicle. Most vehicle owners are also environmentally conscious, not because the two go together, but because car ownership is so wide that the non-driving 'idealist' is a rarity.

In the 1960s, despite the public appeals made by Ralph Nader and his supporters in the US and UK, car safety would not sell. As traffic densities and potential maximum speed levels have increased over the years, the importance of safety has resonated with people, in a way which the appalling accident statistics did not, and safety devices are now a key part of media advertising for cars. Traffic densities are also now high enough to make the *problems of pollution* strike-home to a much greater extent.

The price premium necessary for electric-drive vehicles is not necessarily an intrinsic one, merely the price one has to pay for goods of relatively low volume manufacture, in the case of specialist EVs. However, the torque characteristics of electric motors potentially allow for less complex vehicles to be built, often without change-speed gearboxes and without differential gearing, drive-shafting, clutch and final-drive gears, pending the availability of cheaper materials with the appropriate electromagnetic properties. Complex ignition and fuel-injection systems disappear alongside the conventional IC engine, together with the balancing problems of converting reciprocating motion to rotary motion within the piston engine. The exhaust system with its complex pollution controllers also disappears, along with the difficult mounting problems for a fire-hazardous petrol tank.

These absences also offer greater aesthetic-design freedom to stylists. Obviating the need for firewall bulkheads, and thick acoustic insulation, also allows greater scope in vehicle interior design, in appealing to potential buyers. The public has demonstrated its wish for wider choice of bodywork and the lightweight 'punt' type structure becoming of wider interest gives the stylist almost as much freedom as had the traditional body-builders who constructed custom body designs on the vehicle manufacturers' running chassis.

The ability of the punt structure, to hang its doors from cantilevered A-and C-posts without a centre pillar, provides considerable freedom of side access, and the ability to use seat swivelling and sliding mechanisms to ease access, promises a good sales point for a multi-stop urban vehicle. The resulting platform can support a variety of body types, including open-sports and sports-utility, as no roof members need be involved in the overall structural integrity. Most important, though, is the freedom to mount almost any configuration of non-structural plastic bodywork for maximum stylistic effect. The alternative approach by Gordon Murray Design uses a space-frame structure for his T.25 and T.27 cars, made from laser cut and laser welded box-sectioned steel tube, and stiffened by a composite floor panel. The body front section is hinged on this frame and opens forward to allow easy access for passengers past the centrally mounted driver's seat.

Somehow, too, the stylist and his marketing colleagues have to see that there is a realization among EV buyer prospects that only when a petrol engine runs at wide open-throttle at about 75% of its maximum rotational speed is it achieving its potential 25% efficiency; this is of course only for very short durations in urban, or high density traffic, situations. It is suggested that a large-engine car will average less that 3% efficiency over its life while a small-engine car might reach 8%, one of the prices paid for using the IC engine as a variable speed and power source. Of course, this disadvantage is offset by the very high calorific value packed by a litre of petrol and, in the case of an advanced Gordon Murray car, by using a maximum-efficiency very high-revving motor-cycle-type engine, without flywheel, and in conjunction with a ten-speed gearbox.

However, an electric car has potential for very low cost per mile operation based on electrical recharge costs for the energy-storage batteries, and EVs are potentially competitive even when the cost of battery replacement is included after the limit of charge/recharge cycles has been reached. It needs to be made apparent to the public that a change in batteries is akin to changing the cartridge in a photocopier: essentially the 'fuel package' is renewed while the remainder of the car platform (machine) has the much longer life, normally associated with electric-drive than with the petrol-driven vehicle. In this sense batteries are amortizable capital items, to be related with the much longer replacement period for the vehicle platform which could well carry different body styles during its overall lifetime.

The over-sizing of petrol engines in conventional cars, referred to above, is due to several factors. Typical car masses, relative to the masses of the drivers they carry, mean that less than 2% of fuel energy is used in carrying the driver. The specifying of engines that allow cars to travel at very large margins above the maximum speed limit, is of course, the result of conventional construction techniques and materials that make cars comparatively heavy. The weight itself, of course, grossly affects accelerative performance and gradient ability. Also some estimates consider six units of fuel are needed to deliver one unit of energy to the wheels: one-third wheel power being lost in acceleration (and heat in consequent braking), one-third in heating disturbed air as the vehicle pushes through the atmosphere and one-third in heating the tyre and road at the traction, braking and steering contact-patch. This puts priorities on design for electric vehicles to cut tare weight, reduce aerodynamic drag and reduce tyre rolling resistance.

Near-future opportunities for EVs, from press reports

An example of new approaches to 'ownership' for EV users has been reported in the Autolib system introduced in Paris based on the electric Bluecar. By 2013 it is forecast that some 5000 such vehicles will be in use in the city, according to press reports. The Paris mayor is convinced that car-sharing will be the future for automobile traffic in cities and hence the pay-as-you-go Autolib system. The Bluecar 4-seater is capable of 0-100 km/hour acceleration in 6.7 seconds after an 8-hour plug-in charge, which will give it a range of 250 km. Hire-prices range from £10 to £144 per year depending on the length of time the car is used.

In Britain specialist vehicle producers, of all vehicle types, are numerically strong and it is encouraging to find that engineers from the UK Motor Industry Research Association (MIRA) have worked alongside one of these, Warwickshire-based Gevco (Global Electric Vehicle Company), to produce a prototype long-range electric car concept that it is hoped will be taken up by a number of small-to-medium car-makers, which would share investment costs and customise the design for particular specialist market sectors in the course of the next five years. The gradual expansion of the technology park at MIRA, near Nuneaton, might be a location for firms seeking to set up premises for EV propulsion system development. It is reported that MIRA's growth plan could create a total of 2000 jobs at the technology park, in its suppliers and in its own laboratories. EV propulsion systems also present opportunities for development, with the reported case of lithium-air batteries having ten times the energy storing potential over the more commonly used lithium-ion battery.

London's gradual introduction of zero-emission vehicles might have been just before the 2012 Olympic Games with the destined introduction of two fuel-cell/battery hybrid taxis produced in a joint enterprise between Intelligent Energy, LTI, Lotus Engineering and TRW Conekt. The fuel cell net power output of the prototype was 30kW in 2010 and the unit was fuelled by 3.7 kg of hydrogen stored in a 154 litre tank pressure-charged to 35 MPa. The Lithium Ion battery pack has a capacity of 15kWh to drive the 55kW motor when the vehicle is in battery mode; the fuel cell mode is said to be good for a 5000 hours operational life (around 150,000 miles). As an electric hybrid the range is 160 miles and top speed 81 mile/h.

The rewards of current vehicle weight reduction programmes are made evident, however, by the example of McLaren's high-performance MP4-12C sports car project destined for a production volume of 1000 units per year. Following racing-car practice carbon-fibre is the key (monocell) component of the vehicle structure. In this case it weighs less than 80kg but is 25% stiffer than the equivalent metal structure. The rear end of the car is a sacrificial aluminium alloy structure to absorb crash loads in impact and support the engine. The whole car weighs 1300 kg which is highly competitive for this class of vehicle, powered by a 600 bhp engine, and every small component of the car was subject to intensive weight-saving treatment. In the McLaren chief designer's own company, Gordon Murray Design, remarkable progress has been made in ultra light weight city-car prototypes, powered by petrol engines.

Developments for farther future EV operation, from press reports

As emphasised by the horrific motorway 'pile-up' of vehicles in Somerset, UK, at the end of 2011, there is a need for a host of safety options for passenger and drivers. One hope is the 'hands-off' vehicle electronic guidance systems under evaluation for motorway use. There is prospect of a system of self-steering vehicles (with their 'drivers' seated with hands-off the steering wheels), which are directionally controlled by the vehicle ahead, in a train guided by a human-controlled leader-vehicle. The early stages of this has been successfully demonstrated by Ricardo and its Swedish clients as part of the pan-European Sartre project which is scheduled to deliver its findings in mid-2012. The so-called 'platooning' offers benefits in terms of congestion and fuel economy as well as road safety.

Each convoy, or platoon, would be controlled by a leading 'coach', driven by a professional driver, which would monitor the behaviour of the cars behind it. Sensors such as radar, camera and laser would keep the cars spaced at about five metres apart and positioned by a steer-by-wire or similar system. The first successful demonstration of the system has taken place at the Volvo proving ground in Sweden, with a single 'trailing' car and leader vehicle at 30 mile/h and tests of a five car platoon were made at the end of 2011; the whole Sartre programme is due to report in 2013. Perhaps a medium sized partner-firm might be able to develop such a system for commercial acceptance. If the platoon leader could be an electric vehicle controlled, and perhaps one day inductively powered, by a buried-wire inductive/guidance system, even a fully automated train of EVs could possibly be developed in future years that might take the fatigue away from motorway driving, and even ease the transition on to branch A-roads.

Yet farther future pure-electric and hybrid vehicles might benefit from fuel cells, super-capacitors and small gas turbines. In 2008 Transport for London and the Technology Strategy Board addressed the problem of London's 20,000 'black cabs' described as having noisy and polluting diesel engines, said to give the capital one of the worst polluting levels among European capitals. These two organisations funded a £1 million project for developing 20 zero-emission taxis, based on the LTI TX4 cab in time for the 2012 London Olympics.

Two fuel-cell powered prototypes were demonstrated to the press in August 2010 on the Lotus test track. Each had a 154-litre front-mounted hydrogen tank adjacent to the fuel cell, but with minimum change to the standard cab specification. The fuel cell supplier, Intelligent Energy, was hoping to achieve a 40,000 hour life for the cell. London mayor Johnson had promised six London hydrogen-refuelling stations by the opening of the Olympics.

Other contenders for the Olympics cab launch include Eco City based on the Vito Mercedes cab. The E-Vito was claimed to have a 120 mile range on one battery charge. The existing Vito cab had won 30% of the new purchases market and the E-Vito, with a 70 kW power-train by Zytec, who developed the vehicle in conjunction with Advantage West Midlands, which funded the project, also Penso, a Coventry company, battery supplier Valence, Mercedes and One80.

The miniaturisation of gas turbines by the British firm Bladon Jets produced an axial flow turbine as a highly efficient alternative to the IC engine that presumably has potential to run off hydrogen stored on a hybrid vehicle with a fuel-cell prime power-unit. The company had been due to lead a £2.2 million project funded by the Technology Strategy Board for future generations of electric vehicles. The range-extender will also incorporate a high-speed generator using switched reluctance technology by SR Drives, and involved vehicle integrator Jaguar Land Rover. The gas-turbine/generator is able to run continuously at its optimum speed, with any excess power available for battery charging, and has weight savings of up to 10% claimed against a conventional IC-engine vehicle, with the added advantage of much faster warm-up times.

New Ways for Indigenous Manufacturing

Materials researchers at Imperial College in 2010 announced a prototype material, with potential for electrical energy storage, which the college considered could turn around the negative perception, by some, of the range and weight of electric vehicles. This has been revealed in a £3.4 million EU funded project named 'Storage'. Major car panels made from a unique carbon filled sandwich enclosing a glass-fibre core can be electrically charged to store energy, which can charged and discharged much quicker than a conventional battery and effect an estimated 15% reduction of electric vehicle weight. The UK company, Umeco, of the Advanced Composite Group were reportedly interested in mass-production of the material and much higher weight savings are forecast for EVs.

The WiTricity Corporation, of Watertown, Massachusetts, USA, is reportedly developing technology for wireless charging of electric vehicles. Based on magnetic induction and is able to charge a primary electricity source up to one metre away. The technology was originally researched at M.I.T. for range extension by fine-tuning the design of the magnetic coils that generate oscillating magnetic fields.

APPENDIX B

US transplants, set up in the UK, and US acquisitions of UK auto-components businesses

Year:	Products:	US Corporation:	Acquired concerns or transplants
1960s	Automatic transmission	Borg Warner	(Letchworth and Kenfig)
1960s	Diesel engine	Cummins	[Shotts and Darlington]
1960s	Transmission components	American Twin-Disk	[UK]
1962	Transmission gearboxes	Eaton	ENV
1967	Radiator systems	Kysor	[Rochdale]
1968	Engineering-rubber products	Goodyear	[Craigavonj
1968	Bostrom vehicle seats	Universel Oil Product	[Northhampton]
1966	CV brakes	Rockwell	Centrax Gears
1969	In-car entertainment systems	Motorola	[Stotfold]
1969	CV drive axles	Rockwell	Rubery-Owen
1969	Trim texturing	Standard International	J Martin & Sons
1970	Fasteners	Aircraft Marine Products	[Bideford]

New Ways for Indigenous Manufacturing

Year:	Products:	US Corporation:	Acquired concerns or transplants
1971	Diesel engines	Detroit Diesel	[Northants]
1971	Turbochargers	Garrett Air Research	[Skelmersdale]
1971	Vehicle hydraulics	Rexroth	[St Neots]
1971	Clutches	Dana Spicer	Turner Man'ing
1972	Power Steering	Eaton	Hobourn Man'ing
1972	Gearshifts	Teleflex Morse	[Basildon]
1972	Aeon rubber springs	Firestone	[North London]
1972	Clutches	Lipe-Roliway	[Rossendale]
1973	Exhaust silencers	Tenneco-Walker	[Belfast]
1973	Automotive plastics	Du Pont	[Hemel Hempstead]
1973	Gaskets/adhesives	Dow Corning	[Reading]
1976	Die-cast components	Chrysler	Hills Precision
1976	Brake systems	Bendix-Westinghouse	[Bristol]
1977	Axles	Eaton	Rubery-Owen
1977	Hydraulic hose	Aeroquip	{Reddich]
1977	Seats	Sears	Coventry Motor Systems
1979	Electro-plating	3M	[Atherstone]
1981	Chassis pressings	Rockwell	Rubery Owen
1981	Hydraulic systems	Sunstrand	Plessey Hydraulics
1982	Adhesives	Fasson	[Cramlington]
1982	Transmissions	Dana Spicer	[Wolverhampton]
1982	Body components	Rockwell	Wilmot Breeden
1982	Power presses	Verson International	Wilkins & Mitchell
1963	Automotive CAD	Computervision	Cambridge Interactive Systems
1983	Body assembly systems	Lamb Technicon	Sceptre Engineering

New Ways for Indigenous Manufacturing

Year:	Products:	US Corporation:	Acquired concerns or transplants
1963	Vehicle trim products	DL Auld	Joseph Fray
1983	Automotive paints	Berger	[Dagenham]
1964	Axles and hydraulics	Hydreco-Hamworthy	[Southampton]
1964	Fasteners	TRW	United Carr
1964	Fan drive systems	Eaton	Holset Engineering
1985	Paints	PPG Industries	International Paints
1985	Suspension systems	Hendrickson International	Norde Suspensions
1965	Plastics parts	Uniroyal	[Edinburgh]
1966	Kevlar composites	Du Pont	[Londonderry]
1966	Engine development	Fuel Tech	Engineering Research & Application
1966	Pressings	Rockwell	Thompson Pressings
1966	ABS systems	Bendix	Anti Skid Controls lid
1987	Electronic systems	Ford	[Dundee]
1966	Automotive semiconductors	Motorola	[Stotfold]
1986	Seat belt systems	Allied Signal	Kangol
1966	Occupant restraint systems	TRW	[Peterlee]
1986	Vehicle electrics	Prestolite	Butec Electrics
1969	Switches	TRW	[Sunderland]
1969	Active suspension	Monroe	Lotus Engineering
1989	Sunroofs	Rockwell Golde	[Birmingham]
1990	Suspension dampers	Monroe	Armstrong Patents
1990	Timing belts	Gates Rubber	[Dumfries]
1990	Air brake components	WABCO	[Leeds]

New Ways for Indigenous Manufacturing

Year:	Products:	US Corporation:	Acquired concerns or transplants
1990	Automatic chassis lubrication	Denco	Telelube
1991	Computer-aided engineering	AT&T	Istel
1991	Plastic mouldings	Johnson Controls	Premier Polymer Mouldings
1991	Plastics welding	Branson Ultrasonics	Dawe Ultrasonics
1991	Wiper motors	ITT	[Skelmersdale]
1991	Steering wheels	United Technologies	Clifford Covering Co
1992	Nylons	Du Pont	ICI
1992	Engineering plastics	Polypence	[Birmingham]
1992	Engine valves	TRW	[Tyne & Wear]
1993	Seats	Johnson Controls	[Burton-on-Trent]
1993	Steering components	TRW	JN Kirby Products
1993	Seats	Johnson Controls	[Wolverhampton]
1994	Acrylic resins	Ashland Chemical	ICI
1995	CV air suspension	Neway Anchorlok	[Kidderminster]
1995	On-vehicle electronics	TRW	[Sunderland]
1997	Tyres	Cooper (Ohio)	Avon Tyres lid
1997	Clutch/brake friction linings	'American investors"	Ferodo
1997	Components	Arwin Industries	Timex
1997	Assembly/test systems	DT Industries	Lucas Assembly and Test
1997	Major automotive systems	Federel	Mogul T & N

New Ways for Indigenous Manufacturing

Year:	Products:	US Corporation:	Acquired concerns or transplants
1998	Plastics components	Collins & Aikman Kigass	(Leamington)
1998	Race-car engines	Ford	Cosworth
1996	Plastic components	Textron	Midlands Industrial Plastics
1998	Transmissions	Textron	David Brown
1999	Paints	Du Pont	Herberts
1999	Mirrors	Donnelly Vision GP	(Edinburgh)
1999	Switches	Stoneridge (Ohio)	Delta Schoeller (UK)
1999	Automotive systems	Walbra	TI Group
1999	Paints	PPG Industries	ICI
2000	Automotive electronics	Ford (Visteon)	Pi Technology
2000	Aftermarket parts	Delphi	AP Group
2001	Dashboard instrument displays	Walbra	Smiths Industries
2001	Components	Delco Remy International	XL Component Distribution
2001	Drive axles	American Axle & Manufacturing	Albion Automotive

APPENDIX C

Graphs figured in main text

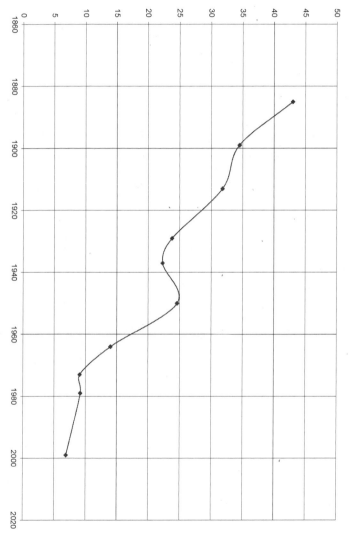

Fig. 1 UK percentage share in world trade of manufactured goods

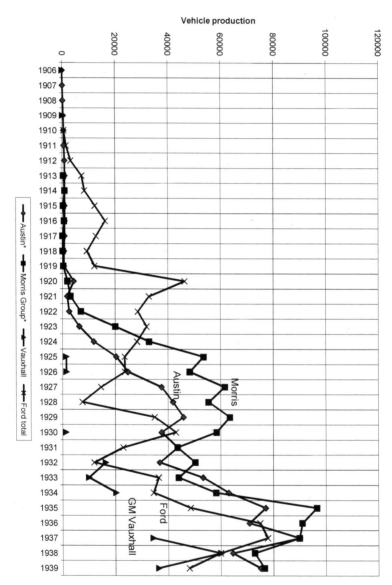

Fig.2: UK indigenous and transplant volume car makers' units produced in 1906-1939

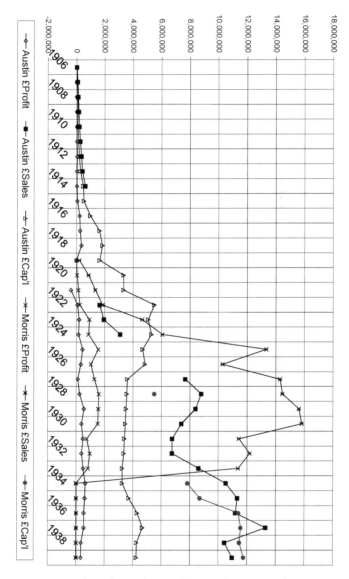

Fig.3: Profit, sales and capital in £s of Austin and Morris

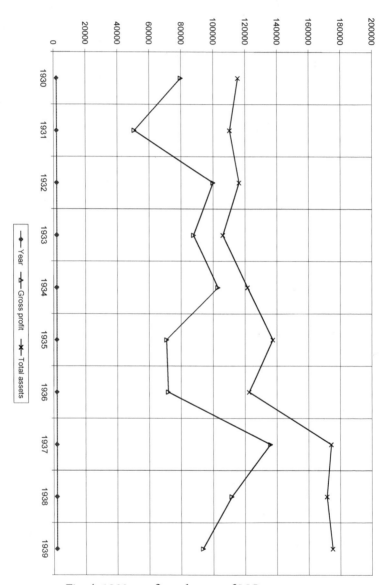

Fig. 4: 1930s profit and assets of MG car company

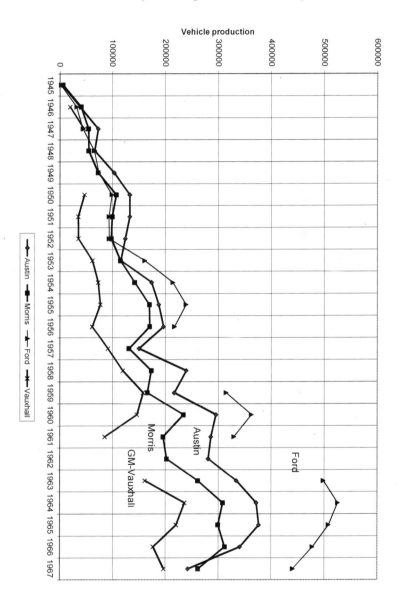

Fig. 5: Individual production figures for Ford, Austin, Morris and GM

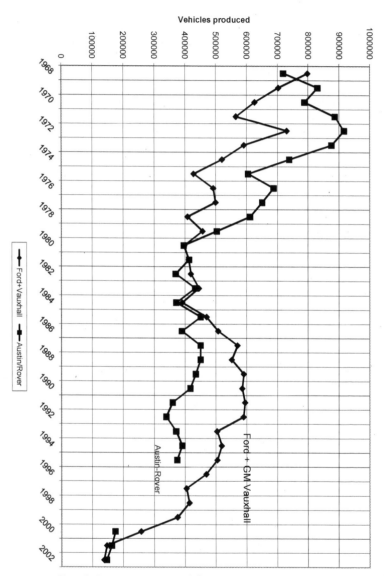

Fig. 6: Outputs compared for Austin/Rover and Ford plus GM Vauxhall

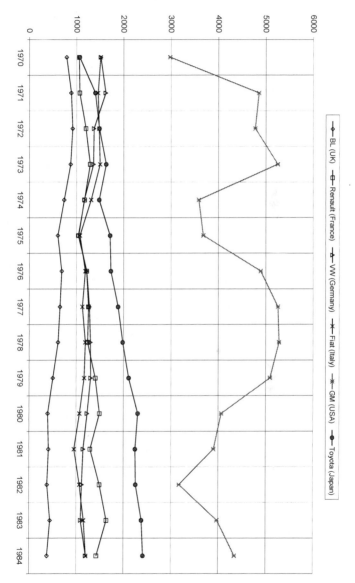

Fig. 7: Car output (thousands of units) from main indigenous national firms

APPENDIX D

Tables figured in the main text

Table 1: Phases of productivity growth (GDP/ man-hour)

. . . from Gamble (1985, Table 1.2)

	1870-1913	*1913-50*	*1950-76*
France	1.8	1.7	4.9
Germany	1.9	1.2	5.8
Italy	1.2	1.8	5.3
Japan	1.8	1.4	7.5
United States	2.1	2.5	2.3
United Kingdom	1.1	1.5	2.8

Source: A. Maddison, 'The Long Run Dynamics of Productivity Growth', in W. Beckerman (ed.) *Slow Growth in Britain* (Oxford University Press, 1979) p. 195.

Table 2: Percentage of net earnings retained by 'Big Six' car makers

	1929-33	1934-8	1947-56	1952-6
Morris	50	25	39	
Austin	33	31	72	
[BMC				68]
Standard	80	40	52	
Rootes			79	
Ford	20	23	79	
Vauxhall	72	42	74	

Table 3. Rates of return on capital of the 'Big Six' car makers

	1929	1930	1931	1932	1933	1934	1935	1936	1937	1938
Morris	16	17	11	12	6	8	15	19	16	12
Austin	21	25	9	14	15	18	16	15	16	11
Standard	loss	19	24	48	27	19	25	23	26	9
Humber	loss	4	loss	loss	7	22	14	14	14	8
Ford	12	11	3	loss	loss	7	4	6	5	3
Vauxhall	n/a	n/a	12	18	41	54	58	47	32	24

REFERENCES

Introduction

0.1 Collins & Robbins, Eds., *British Culture and Economic Decline*, Weidenfeld & Nicolson, 1990, final chapter

0.2 Gamble, A, *Britain in decline*, Macmillan, 2nd edition, 1985 (pp. 26-32)

0.3 Veblen, T, *The Theory of the Leisure Class,* [1899], Penguin edition 1994, pp. 22-34, 188-211

0.4 Hilferding, R, *Finance Capital*, Routledge & Keegan Paul, 1981 trans of 1910 original, pp. 107-118

0.5 Blair, M, *Ownership and Control: Rethinking Corporate Governance for the Twenty-first Century,* The Brookings Institution, Washington, D.C., 1995 (pp. 1-13, 37-42, 103-106, 223-5)

0.6 Ekelund & Tollison, *Microeconomics: Private Market and Public Choice*, Addison Wesley, 1981

0.7 Williams, R, *Culture and Society*, 1780-1950, Hogarth Press, pp. xvi-xviii, 1987

0.8 Barker, C, *Cultural Studies, Theory and Practice*, Sage, 2004 (pp. 156-161)

0.9 Jessop, B, *Thatcherism and Flexibility: the White Heat of a post-Fordist Revolution*, in Jessop et al (eds.) *The Politics of Flexibility*, Edward Elgar, 1991 (pp. 19-20)

0.10 Jessop, B, *Post-Fordism and the State*, Chapter 8 in Amin (ed.), *Post Fordism*, Blackwell, 1996

0.11 Brown, J, *The Social Psychology of Industry*, Pelican, 1965

0.12 Hutton, W, *Them and Us*, Little, Brown, 2010

0.13 Hutton, W, *The State We're In,* Vintage, 1996

0.14 Nieuwenhuis and Wells, Car Futures - rethinking the automotive industry beyond the American model, www.trendtracker.co.uk

0.15 Macmillan, H, *Winds of Change, 1914-1939,* Macmillan, 1966

0.16 Jenkins, R, *Churchill,* Pan Books, 2001

Chapter 1

1.1. Clare Tomalin, *Samuel Pepys, the Unequalled Self,* Penguin, 2003

1.2. John Keay, *The Honourable Company,* Harper Collins, 1991

1.3. Smith, A, *The Wealth of Nations,* W Strahan & T Cadell, London, 1776

1.4. David Landes, D, *The Unbound Prometheus,* Cambridge University Press, 1969 (pp. 190-2)

1.5. Mathias, P, *The First Industrial Nation,* second edition, Methuen, 1983 (pp. 323-354)

1.6. Gamble, A, *Britain in Decline,* Macmillan, 2nd edition, 1985 (pp. 68-76)

1.7 Bronowski and Mazlish, *The Western Intellectual Tradition,* Harper Collins, 1960

1.8 Barnett, C, *The Collapse of British Power,* Pan Books, 1972

1.9 Garfield, S, *The Last Journey of William Huskisson,* Faber and Faber, 2003

1.10 Hill, CP, *British Economic and Social History 1700-1975,* 4th Edition, Arnold, 1977

1.11 David Cannadine, *Aspects of Aristocracy,* Penguin, 1994

1.12 Lane, P, *The Upper Class,* Batsford, 1972

1.13 Hamnett et al, eds., *The Changing Social Structure,* Sage, 1989 (pp 163-216)

1.14 Joyce, P, Essay entitled *Work* in Chapter 3 of Thompson, F, (ed.), *Cambridge Social History of Great Britain,* Vol 2, Cambridge, 1990 (pp. 131-194)

1.15. Stana Nenadic, *Businessmen, the Urban Middle Classes, and the 'Dominance' of Manufacturers in Nineteenth Century Britain*, Economic History Review, 44, 1(1991), pp 66-85

1.16 Coleman, D, *Gentlemen and Players*, Economic History Review, XXVI, 1, pp. 92-116

1.17. Asa Briggs, *Victorian People*, Penguin, 1990 (pp. 124-147)

1.18. Martin Wiener, *English Culture and the Decline of the Industrial Spirit*, Penguin, 1992

1.19. Bronowski and Mazlish, *The Western Intellectual Tradition*, Harper Collins, 1960 (pp. 280-356)

1.20 Williams, R, *Culture and Society*, 1780-1950, Hogarth Press, 1987 (pp xiii-xx)

1.21 Levine, A, *Industrial Retardation in Britain*, 1880-1914, Weidenfeld and Nicolson, 1967

1.22 Eldridge et al, in *The Mass Media Power in Modern Britain*, Oxford University Press, 1997

1.23 WJ Reader, *The Middle Classes*, Batsford, 1972

1.24 Wrigley, C, *Lloyd George*, Blackwell, 1992

1.25 Barnett, C, *The Collapse of British Power*, Papermac, Pan Books, 1972

1.26 Walker, W, *A History of the Oundle Schools*, The Grocers Company, 1956

1.27 McKendrick, N. in his introduction to Church's *Herbert Austin and the British Motor Industry until 1941*, Europa publications, 1979

1.28. Eric Hobsbawm, *Industry and Empire*, Weidenfeld and Nicholson, 1968

1.29. Briggs, A *The English: Custom and Character*, in Ed. Robert Blake, *The English World*, 1982

1.30 Cole & Postgate, *The Common People: 1746-1946*, Methuen, 1971 (pp. 415-425, 458-542)

1.31 Marquand, D, *Britain since 1918*, Weidenfeld & Nicolson, 2008 (pp. 117-120, 108-110)

1.32. Glover *et al*, in *Engineering our Future again: Towards a Long-term Strategy for Manufacturing and Management in the*

United Kingdom, Chapter 11 in Eds. Delbridge and Lowe, *Manufacturing in Transition*, Routledge, 1998

1.33 Hill, C, *British Economic and Social History 1700-1975*, 4th Edition, 1977, Arnold

1.34 Cole & Postgate (Op. Cit., pp.616-624, 625-632)

1.35 Coates, D, *Running the country*, Second Edition, Hodder and Stoughton, 1995

1.36 Mathius, P, *The First Industrial Nation*, second edition, Methuen, 1983 (323-354)

1.37 Georgano, N, (Ed.) *Britain's Motor Industry*, Foulis, 1995 (Ch. 2)

1.38 Richardson, K, *The British Motor Industry 1896-1939*, Foulis, 1977 (pp. 7-19)

1.39 Saul, S, 'The Motor Industry in Britain to 1914', *Business History*, V, no. 1, 1962

1.40 Sampson, A, *The Changing Anatomy of Britain*, Coronet Books, pp. 462-76, 1983

Chapter 2

2.1 Barnett, C, *The Audit of War*, Papermac, 1987

2.2 Turner, G, The Car Makers, Pelican, 1964

2.3 Piore and Sabel, *Mass Production as Destiny and Blind Decision*, Chapter 2 in *The Second Industrial Divide*, Basic Books, New York, 1984 (pp. 231)

2.4 Piore and Sabel, *Mass Production as Destiny and Blind Decision*, Chapter 2 in *The Second Industrial Divide*, Basic Books, New York, 1984 (pp. 5-6, 19-21)

2.5 Lambert and Wyatt, *Lord Austin, the Man*, Sidgwick and Jackson, 1968

2.6 Church, R, *The Rise and Decline of the British Motor Industry*, 1994 (pp. 27, 55, 72)

2.7 Tolliday, S, and Zeitlin, J, *The Automobile Industry and its Workers*, Polity Press, 1986

New Ways for Indigenous Manufacturing

2.8 Bowden & Turner, *Determinants of the Diffusion of Car Ownership in the Inter-War UK Economy*, Business History, V. 35, N. 1, 1993 (pp. 55-69)

2.9 Jessop, B, *Thatcherism and Flexibility: the White Heat of a post-Fordist Revolution*, in Jessop et al (eds.) *The Politics of Flexibility*, Edward Elgar, 1991 (pp. 19-20)

2.10 Braverman, H, *Labour and Monopoly Capitalism: the Degradation of Work in the Twentieth Century*, Monthly Review Press, 1974

2.11 Sloan, A, *My Years with General Motors*, Macfadden, 1965

2.12 Elbaum and Lazonick, *The Decline of the British Economy: an Institutional Perspective.* Journal of Economic History, Vol XLIV, No 2, June 1984 (pp. 657-683)

2.13 Tolliday, S, and Zeitlin, J, *The Automobile Industry and its Workers*, Polity Press, 1986

2.14 Church, R, *The Rise and Decline of the British Motor Industry*, 1994 (pp. 21)

2.15 Jessop, B, *Thatcherism and Flexibility: the White Heat of a post-Fordist Revolution*, in Jessop et al (eds.) *The Politics of Flexibility*, Edward Elgar, 1991 (pp. 19-20)

2.16 Coates, D, *Running the country*, Second Edition, Hodder and Stoughton, 1995

2.17 Jessop, B, *Thatcherism and Flexibility: the White Heat of a post-Fordist Revolution*, in Jessop et al (eds.) *The Politics of Flexibility*, Edward Elgar, 1991 (pp. 19-20)

2.17 Simms & Boyle, Eminent Corporations: the Rise and Fall of the Great British Corporation, Constable & Robinson, 2010

2.18 Mathius, P, *The First Industrial Nation*, second edition, Methuen, 1983 (323-354)

2.19 Glover I, Tracey, P, Currie, W, *Engineering our Future again: Towards a Long-term Strategy for Manufacturing and Management in the United Kingdom*, Chapter 11 in Eds. Delbridge and Lowe, *Manufacturing in Transition*, Routledge, 1998

2.20 Cole & Postgate, *The Common People: 1746-1946*, Methuen, 1971 (pp. 415-425, 458-542)

New Ways for Indigenous Manufacturing

2.21 Stevenson, J, (Op. Cit. pp. 43, 103-142)

2.22 Mathius, P, *The First Industrial Nation*, second edition, Methuen, 1983 (323-354)

2.23 Sampson, A, *Company Men,* Harper Collins, 1995

2.24 Jones, G, *Foreign Multinationals and British Industry before 1945*, Economic History Review, 2nd ser., XLI, 3 (1988), pp. 429-453.

2.25 Magee, G, *Manufacturing and Technological Change*, Chapter 4 in Eds Floud, R, and Johnson, P, *The Cambridge Economic History of modern Britain*, Vol 2 *Economic Maturity,* 1860-1939, Cambridge, 2004 (pp. 74-98)

2.26 Foreman-Peck, J, *The American Challenge of the Twenties: Multinationals and the European Motor Industry*, Journal of Economic History, V. 42, 1982 (pp. 865-881)

2.27 Piore and Sabel, *Mass Production as Destiny and Blind Decision*, Chapter 2 in *The Second Industrial Divide*, Basic Books, New York, 1984 (pp. 5-6, 19-21)

2.28 Mackie, R, *Family ownership and business survival: Kirkaldy, 1870-1970, Business History*, Vol. 43 Issue 3, pp.1-32, Jul 2001 (pp. 1-32)

2.29 Knowles *et al, op. cit. The Industrial and commercial Revolutions in Great Britain during the Nineteenth Century*, Routledge, 1941

2.30 Mathius, P, *The First Industrial Nation*, second edition, Methuen, 1983 (323-354, 366-384)

2.31 Freeman & Jones, *Technological Trends and Employment: Engineering and Vehicles,* Gower, 1985

2.32 Kirby, MW, *Institutional Rigidities and economic Decline: Reflections on the British Experience*, The Economic History review, New Series, V.45, N.4, 1992 (pp. 637-660)

2.33 May, J, *An economic and social history of Britain 1760-1970,* 1972 (pp. 349-351)

2.34 Marquand, D, *Britain since 1918*, Weidenfeld & Nicolson, 2008 (pp. 117-12, 108-110)

2.35 Kidd and Nicholls, *The Making of the British Middle Class*, Sutton Publishing, (1998, pp. xv, xxx, xxxviii).

2.36 Orwell, G, Published in The Collected Essays, *Journalism and Letters of George Orwell*, Vol 2 *My Country Right or Left*, 1940-1943, Penguin, 1970, 1 (1970, 1, pp. 77, 87, 88-99, 242)

2.37 Stevenson, J, *British Society: 1914-1945*, Pelican, 1984 (pp. 29, 21-45)

2.38 Wiener, M, *English Culture and the Decline of the Industrial Spirit*, Penguin, 1992

2.39 Cannadine, D, *Class in Britain*, Yale University Press, 1998

2.40 Williams, F, *Dangerous Estate*, Longmans, Green, 1957

2.41 Coates, D, *Running the country*, Second Edition, Hodder and Stoughton, 1995

2.42 Cole & Postgate, *The Common People: 1746-1946*, Methuen, 1971 (pp. 544-567, 656-7)

2.43 Cole & Postgate (Ibid. pp.616-624)

2.44 Mackie, R, *Family ownership and business survival: Kirkaldy, 1870-1970, Business History*, Vol. 43 Issue 3, pp.1-32, Jul 2001 (pp. 1-32)

2.45 Mathius, P, *The First Industrial Nation*, second edition, Methuen, 1983 (323-354)

2.46 Simms & Boyle, *Eminent Corporations: the Rise and Fall of the Great British Corporation*, Constable & Robinson, 2010

2.47 Hobsbawm (Op. Cit., pp 26, 151, 183)

Chapter 3

3.0 Barnett, C, *The Verdict of Peace*, Pan Books, 2003

3.1 Wood, J, Chap 6, *Export or Die*, in Georgano, N, (Ed.) *Britain's Motor Industry*, Foulis, 1995

3.2 Williams, K. et al, *The Breakdown of Austin Rover: a case study in the failure of business strategy and industrial policy*, Berg, 1987 (pp. 112-113)

3.3 Kynaston, D, *A World to Build*, Bloomsbury Publishing, 2008

3.4 Kynaston, D, *Family Britain, 1951-57*, Bloomsbury, 2010

3.5 Elliot & Jacobson, *Longbridge - the Great Survivor*, Vehicle Engineer, Vol. 12, No. 2 - Vol. 18, No. 2-5, 2000-2006

3.6 Fenton, J, *Automotive Body and Systems Design*, Professional Engineering Publishing, 1998

3.7 Church, R, *Historical foundations of corporate culture: British Leyland, its predecessors and Ford*, Chap. 7 in Godley & Westall, *Business History and Business Culture*, Manchester U.P.,1996

3.8 Rhys, D, *The Motor Industry: An Economic Survey*, Butterworth, 1972

3.9 Steven Tolliday, *Competition and the Workplace in the British Automobile Industry. 1945-1988*, *Business and Economic History*, Series 2, Vol. 17, 1988.

3.10 Simms & Boyle, Eminent Corporations: the Rise and Fall of the Great British Corporation, Constable & Robinson, 2010

3.11 Church, R, *The Rise and Decline of the British Motor Industry*, 1994 (pp. 92-106)

3.12 Rowthorn, R, *International big business, 1957-1967, a study of comparative growth,* Cambridge University Press, 1971 (pp. 1-5)

3.13 Ohmae, K, *The Rise of the Region State,* Foreign Affairs, Vol 72, No 2, 78-87, 1993 (pp. 78-87)

3.14 Aw and Chatterjee, *The performance of UK firms acquiring large cross-border and domestic take-over targets*, Cambridge University Judge Institute of Management Studies, 2001

3.15 Williams *et al (op. cit. 3.2)*

3.16 Bostock and Jones, *Foreign Multinationals in 'British Manufacturing, 1850-1962*, Business History, V.36, Issue 1, pp. 89-126, 1994

3.17 Jones, G, *Foreign Multinationals and British Industry before 1945*, Economic History Review, 2nd ser., XLI, 3 (1988), pp. 429-453.

3.18 Kynaston, D, *Family Britain, 1951-57*, Bloomsbury, 2010

3.19 Hewison, R, *Culture and Consensus*, Methuen, 1995 (pp. 88-9, 191)

3.20 Richardson, K, *The British Motor Industry 1896-1939*, Foulis, 1977 (pp. 7-19)

3.21 Coates, D, *Running the country*, Second Edition, Hodder and Stoughton, 1995

3.22 Parker et al, *The sociology of industry*, George Allen and Unwin, 1967

3.23 Wood, Chap. 9, *Decline, then revival*, in Georgano, (Ed.) *Britain's Motor Industry*, Foulis, 1995

3.24 Schenk, C, *Exchange Controls and Multinational Enterprise: the Sterling-Dollar Oil Controversy in the 1950s*, Business History, Vol. 38, No. 4, pp. 21-40, 1996

3.25 Whisler, T, *The British Motor Industry, 1945-1994*, Oxford, 1999

3.26 Church, R, *The Rise and Decline of the British Motor Industry*, 1994 (pp. 92-106)

3.27 Elliot & Jacobson, *Longbridge - the Great Survivor*, Vehicle Engineer, Vol. 12, No. 2 - Vol. 18, No. 2-5, 2000-2006

3.28 Whisler *(op. cit. 3.25)*

3.29 Clausager, Chap. 7, *The Swinging Sixties* in Georgano *Britain's Motor Industry*, Foulis, 1995

3.30 Williams, K. et al, *The Breakdown of Austin Rover: a case study in the failure of business strategy and industrial policy*, Berg, 1987 (pp. 112-113)

3.31 Dunnett, J, *The Decline of the British Motor Industry, The Effects of Government Policy, 1945-1979*, Croom Helm, 1980 (pp. 127-161)

3.32 Mair, A, *From British Leyland Motor Corporation to Rover Group: the Search for a Viable British Model,* Birkbeck College Dept of Management Paper 98/03

3.33 Marquand, D, *Britain since 1918*, Weidenfeld & Nicolson, 2008 (2008, Op. Cit., pp. 111-127)

3.34 Kirby, MW, *Institutional Rigidities and economic Decline: Reflections on the British Experience*, The Economic History review, New Series, V.45, N.4, 1992 (pp. 637-660)

3.35 Marr, *A History of Modern Britain*, Macmillan, Marr (pp. 10-12) 2007

3.36 Kitson & Michie, *Britain's industrial performance since 1960: under-investment and relative decline*, Economic Journal, 106, 1996 (pp. 196-212)

3.37 Coates (1995.1, Op. Cit. pp.61)

3.38 Dahrendorf, R, *On Britain*, BBC Publications, 1982

3.39 Cole & Postgate, *The Common People: 1746-1946*, Methuen, 1971 (pp. 658-72)

3.40 Hall, S, Chapter 8 in English & Kenny (eds.), *Rethinking British Decline*, Macmillan, 104-106, 2000

3.41 Hoggart, R, *Uses of Literacy*, Pelican, 1958 (pp. 53-67)

3.42 Hewison, R, *The Heritage Industry*, Methuen, 1987

3.43 Williams, H, *Britain's Power Elites: the rebirth of a ruling class*, Constable and Robinson, London, 2006, pp. 91, 94

3.44 Hamnett *et al*, eds., *The Changing Social Structure*, Sage, 1989

3.45 Hewison, R, *The Heritage Industry*, Methuen, 1987

3.46 Kynaston D, *Family Britain, 1951-57*, Bloomsbury, 2010

3.47 Williams, H, *Britain's Power Elites: the rebirth of a ruling class*, Constable and Robinson, 2006

3.48 Rae, *The Public School Revolution, Britain's Independent Schools 1964-1979*, Faber & Faber, 1981.

3.49 Alt, J, *The Politics of Economic Decline, Cambridge*, 1979

3.50 Sanderson, M, *The Universities and British Industry, 1850-1970*, Routledge and Kegan Paul, 1972

3.51 Marr, A, *A History of Modern Britain*, Macmillan, 2007 (pp. xxi, 9)

3.52 Fisher, N, *Harold Macmillan*, Weidenfeld and Nicholson, 1982 (pp. 154-159)

3.53 Coates (1995.1, Op. Cit., pp. 82-86)

3.54 May, T, *An economic and social history of Britain, 1760-1990*, Longman, 1995, Chapter 14

3.55 Marwick, A, *Class: Image and Reality*, Collins, 1981, pp 327

3.56 Marwick, A, *British Society since 1945*, Penguin, 1996

3.57 Williams, K *et al*, *Why are the British bad at manufacturing?*, Routledge & Kegan Paul, 1983

3.58 Gamble (1985 Op. Cit. pp. 20-22, pp. 40-42)

3.59 Williams *et al* (1983, Op. Cit., pp. 22, 85-8, 219-263)

3.60 Schenk, (op. cit. 3.24)

New Ways for Indigenous Manufacturing

Chapter 4

4.0   Barnett, C, The Lost Victory, Pan Books, 2002

4.1   Central Policy Review Staff, *The British Motor Industry*, 1975

4.2   Wilks (1990), *Institutional Insularity: government and the British Motor Industry since 1945* in Chick, M, (Ed.) *Governments, Industries and Markets*, Aldershot

4.3   Hutton, W, *The State to Come*, Vintage, 1997

4.4   Church, R, *The Rise and Decline of the British Motor Industry*, 1994 (pp. 92-106)

4.5   Thoms & Donelly, The Coventry motor industry, Ashgate, 2000, (pp 72, 74)

4.6   Edwardes, M, Back from the brink, Pan Books, 1983 (pp.58-60, 79-98, 233-267, 174-196)

4.7   Maxcy, G, *The multi-national motor industry*, Croom Helm, 1981

4.8   Whisler, T, *The British Motor Industry, 1945-1994*, Oxford, 1999

4.9   Mair, A, *From British Leyland Motor Corporation to Rover Group: the Search for a Viable British Model,* Birkbeck College Dept of Management Paper 98/03

4.10 Esser, J, and Hirsch, J, *The Crisis of Fordism and the Dimensions of a 'Post-Fordist' Regional and Urban Structure*, Chapter 3 in Amin (ed.), *Post Fordism*, Blackwell, 1996 (pp. 16-24)

4.11 Broadberry, S, *The Performance of Manufacturing*, Chaper 3 in Floud and Johnson, eds, *The Cambridge Economic History of Modern Britain*, Vol 3, *Structural Change for Growth, 1939-2000*, Cambridge, 2004 (pp. 57)

4.12 Rhys, D, *The Motor Industry: An Economic Survey*, Butterworth, 1972

4.13 Elbaum and Lazonick, Op Cit (pp. 637-660)

4.14 Clausager, Chap. 7, *The Swinging Sixties* in Georgano *Britain's Motor Industry*, Foulis, 1995

4.15 Sampson, A, *Company Men,* Harper Collins, 1995

4.16 May, T, Chapter 15 in *An Economic and Social History of Britain, 1760-1990*, Longman, 1995

4.17 Oughton, C, *Competitive Policy in the 1990s*, Economic Journal, 107:444, pp. 1486-1503, 1997

4.18 Welbourn, D, *Automotive Engineer*, April/May 1990, pp. 21 and *Siemens Review*, No 6/81 (29-32)

4.19 Engineering Manager, Cambridge Silicon Radio

4.20 Collini, S, Introduction to: CP Snow, *The Two Cultures*, Cambridge, 1998

4.21 Hewison, R (1995, Op. Cit.)

4.22 Williams, K et al, *Why are the British bad at manufacturing?*, Routledge & Kegan Paul, 1983

4.23 Bédarida, F, *A social history of England 1851-1990*, Law Book Co of Australasia, 1990

4.24 Church, R, *The Effect of American Multinationals on the British Motor Industry*, in Edsheboyer and Teichova, *Multinationals in Historical Perspective*, Cambridge, 1986

4.25 Savage, M, *The condition of the contemporary middle classes*, essay in Ed. Abercrombie and Wardle, *The Contemporary British Society Reader*, Polity, 2001

4.26 Williams, K et al, *Why are the British bad at manufacturing?*, Routledge & Kegan Paul, 1983

4.27 Marwick, A, *British Society since 1945*, Penguin, 1996

4.28 Hewison, R, *Culture and Consensus*, Methuen, 1995 (pp. 88-9, 191)

4.29 Sanderson, M, *Education and economic decline in Britain, 1870 to the 1990s*, Cambridge University Press, 1999

4.30 Ross, D, *The Unsatisfied Fringe in Britain, 1930s-80s*, Business History, July 1996, Vol. 38 Issue 3, pp. 11-26

4.31 Hutton, W, *The Stakeholding Society*, Polity Press, 1999 (pp. 61-7)

4.32 Marr, A, *A History of Modern Britain*, Macmillan, 2007 (pp.325, 368, 387)

4.33 Dahrendorf, R, *After 1989: Morals, Revolution and Civil Society*

4.34 Coates, D, *Running the country*, Second Edition, Hodder and Stoughton, 1995 (pp. 61)

4.35 Peden, C, *British Economic and Social Policy, Lloyd George to Margaret Thatcher*, Philip Allan, 1991,

4.36 Gamble, A, *Britain in Decline*, Macmillan, 2nd edition, 1985 (pp. 154-158)

4.37 Jessop, B, *Conservative Regimes and the Transition to Post-Fordism: the case of Britain and West Germany*, Essex Papers in Politics and Government, no. 47, University of Essex) 1988 (pp. 84 et seq.)

4.38 Cole & Postgate (Op. Cit., pp.616-624) (pp. 625-632)

4.39 Oughton, C, *Competitive Policy in the 1990s*, Economic Journal, 107:444, pp. 1486-1503, 1997

4.40 Dahrendorf, R, The modern social conflict, an essay on the politics of liberty, Weidenfeld and Nicolson, 1988

4.41 Bostock and Jones, *Foreign Multinationals in British Manufacturing, 1850-1962*, Business History, V.36, Iss. 1, pp. 89-126, 1994

4.42 Lane, C, *Changes in corporate governance of German corporations: convergence to the Anglo-American model?*, Competition and Change, 7, 2-3, 2003 (pp.79-100)

4.43 De Backer, K, and Sleuwaegen, L, *Does foreign direct investment crowd out domestic entrepreneurship?*, Review of Industrial Organisation, V. 22, Iss. 1, pp. 67-84, 2003 (pp. 67-84)

4.44 Kitson & Michie, *Britain's industrial performance since 1960: under-investment and relative decline*, Economic Journal, 106, 1996 (pp. 196-212)

4.45 Lane, C, *Industry and Society in Europe,* Edward Elgar, 1995

4.46 Maxcy, G and Silberston, A, *The Motor Industry*, Allen and Unwin, 1959

4.47 *World Investment Report*, United Nations, 2001

4.48 Bachmann, *Trust, Power and Control in Trans-Organisational Relations*, Organization Studies, 22/2, 2001 (pp. 337-365)

4.49 Lane, C, *Industry and Society in Europe,* Edward Elgar, 1995

4.50 Hall, P and Soskice, D, *An introduction to Varieties of Capitalism*, in Hall & Soskice (eds) *Varieties of Capitalism: the Institutional Foundations of Comparative Advantage*, Oxford University Press, 2001

4.51 Tiratsoo & Tomlinson, *The Conservatives and Industrial Efficiency, 1951-64: Thirteen Wasted Years,* Routledge, 1998

4.52 Peden, C, *British Economic and Social Policy, Lloyd George to Margaret Thatcher*, Philip Allan, (1985/1991, pp. 145),

Chapter 5

5.0 Glancey, J, *The Manual Vanishing, The Guardian*, 23.8.08

5.1 Delbridge and Lowe (eds.), *Manufacturing in Transition*, Routledge, 1998 (pp. 3-4, 22, 24)

5.2 Kitson and Michie, *The political economy of competitiveness*, Routledge, 2000, pp. 111

5.3 Livesey, *Making the most of production*, Cambridge University Institute for Manufacturing, 2003

5.4 Marwick, A, *British Society since 1945*, Penguin, 1996

5.5 Williams, K et al, *Why are the British bad at manufacturing?*, Routledge & Kegan Paul, 1983

5.6 Hutton, W, *Them and Us, Changing Britain - Why we Need a Better Society*, Little, Brown, 2010

5.7 Chatterton & Leonard, *How to avoid the British Disease: Industry in the Eighties*, Northgate Publishing, 1979

5.8 Sanderson, M, *Education and economic decline in Britain, 1870 to the 1990s*, Cambridge University Press, 1999

5.9 Drucker, P, *Post-Capitalist Society*, Harper-Collins, 1994

5.10 Dept of Trade and Industry, *Manufacturing in the knowledge driven economy*, 1999

5.11 Hutton, W, *The World We're in*, Little, Brown, 2002

5.12 Cheffins, B, *History and the Global Corporate Governance Revolution: the UK Perspective*, Business History, V. 43, Iss. 4, Oct. 2001 (pp. 100-118) (pp. 177-9)

5.13 Lane, C, 'Changes in Corporate Governance of German Corporations: convergence to the Anglo-American model?', *Competition and Change*, 7, 2-3, 2003: 79-100

ABOUT THE AUTHOR

John Fenton was recruited into General Motors' first graduate training scheme at its UK Vauxhall subsidiary. After design office experience with the company he moved on to automotive consultants ERA to work as a development engineer on a far reaching vehicle-prototype project for BMC. Later he gained an MSc for research work on commercial-vehicle structures at The College of Aeronautics, Cranfield. From then until his retirement he was involved with the only UK specialist technological-industry magazine circulating within the motor-vehicle industry: *Automotive Design Engineering*, later becoming *Automotive Engineer*, both of which he edited. This 34 year period was punctuated by brief periods of polytechnic teaching, and as product affairs manager for the publicity departments of BL's truck, bus and special-products divisions, both of which provided insight into industrial and educational matters. After retirement he attended a two year 'Access to the Humanities' course at Suffolk College, followed by a three year humanities course at the Open University to gain his BA, in preparation for a five year research period at Birkbeck, University of London from which this book has become the eventual outcome.